SATIRE AND SOCIETY
IN ANCIENT ROME

EXETER STUDIES IN HISTORY

General Editors: Jonathan Barry, MA DPhil
Colin Jones, BA DPhil FRHistS

ROMAN HISTORY TITLES

Roman Political Life 90BC–AD69
edited by T.P. Wiseman

The Administration of the Roman Empire 241BC–AD193
edited by David Braund

Roman Public Buildings
edited by Ian Barton

SATIRE AND SOCIETY
IN ANCIENT ROME

Edited by Susan H. Braund

EXETER STUDIES IN HISTORY No.23
UNIVERSITY OF EXETER

First published 1989 by the University of Exeter

ISBN 0 85989 331 6
ISSN 0260 8626

Exeter University Publications
Reed Hall
Streatham Drive
Exeter EX4 4QR
England

Laserprint origination by Kestrel Data, Exeter
Printed in England by Short Run Press Ltd, Exeter

Contents

Introduction

Roman satire is often used as a source for Roman social history. But the complex nature of satire is not always appreciated either by literary critics or by social historians who sometimes seem to believe that Roman Satire presents a fair and realistic picture of 'everyday life' at Rome. Satire in general tends to distort its subject-matter, especially by selective exaggeration and suppression: exaggeration of shocking, deplorable, disgusting facets of human behaviour and suppression of the boring, mundane and commonplace elements of life. Satire largely consists of the fantastic presentation of extremes, both ideals and hells, so that 'norms' tend to be implicit not explicit. Satire in general tends to simplify, to prefer black and white to shades of grey. Roman Satire is no exception.

This volume contains five essays which suggest how satire can and cannot be used as a source for Roman social history: both opportunities and limitations. The chapters are devoted to themes of prominence and importance in Roman Satire. Of course, such a selection of themes cannot be all-embracing, prescriptive or exclusive. But it is intended that the techniques of analysis presented here will furnish a methodology—or a range of possible methodologies—which will also prove useful when applied to other topics, large and small, in Roman Satire.

First, the historian who wishes to use satire as a source must avoid the biographical fallacy—that is, the identification of poet with the voice we hear speaking in the poems (often called his *persona*, literally 'mask'). An influential victim of this fallacy is Highet 1954 who, in the absence of any reliable external evidence about Juvenal's life,[1] attempts to reconstruct his biography from the poems. This 'biography', given the subject-matter of Juvenal's Satires, can only be colourful. For example, Highet explains Juvenal's apparent misogyny in Satire 6 as the result of 'an unhappy experience with the proud and selfish Roman ladies' (p.103). Green 1960 goes even further, e.g.: 'He had a tender soft spot for children . . . he almost certainly married a lady of society, who treated him abominably . . . he may have become an active paederast . . .' (p.179). Such readings of Juvenal's poems often entail the assumption that Juvenal himself was an impoverished Roman client (material in Satires 1 and 3 especially is used to 'prove' this), but the fact that his poems are dedicated to no patron suggests, on the contrary, that he was not financially dependent. In fact, the first person voice used in the poems (e.g. 'Am I to be a listener only . . .') is just as much a creation of the poet as are his characters who are named; for example, the characters called Priapus and Ofellus created by Horace to deliver Satires 1.8 and 2.2 respectively, the voice of Socrates in Persius' fourth Satire and Juvenal's character Umbricius who utters the long tirade in his third Satire. It is more appropriate to view Roman Satire as a kind of drama which is presented in both monologue and dialogue form; and that is why the concept of the *persona*, 'mask', is so helpful—it reminds us that the poet is not speaking for himself but creating a character.[2]

That the satirists use *personae*, 'masks', is assumed by all five contributors to this volume. An approach which illuminates the distortions of satire is also shared by the first four contributors. This is to use as a 'control' other texts from antiquity; for example, didactic works on farming and medicine and architecture, legal texts, philosophical treatises, and letters which present aspects of the intellectual and social scene at Rome. This of course raises in turn questions about the distortions inherent in the 'control' texts themselves. In other respects the five essays present a wide variety of approaches which illustrate the opportunities and limitations in the use of satire as source material.

In his essay on friendship (*amicitia*), one of the central institutions of Roman society, Mayer immediately raises the crucial issue of perspective —the point of view from which a satirical text is written. He argues that apparently autobiographical material has a primarily moral function and suggests that inconvenient features can be suppressed to produce an idealisation or fantastic scenario which serves the satirist's moral purpose.

Similarly, Braund, using as her starting-point the study of satire from other cultures, emphasises that satirical pictures of city and country are shaped by ideology and invested with symbolism. She suggests other factors which can distort the 'evidence' of satirical texts: the satirist's creation of characters who speak in the poems; the use of parody, literary allusion and wit to entertain the audience; and the influence of the literary tradition of Roman Satire, that is, the 'rules' of the genre, which tend to dictate the presence of certain features and the absence of others.

Cloud's essay on the treatment of law and legal matters in Roman Satire illustrates very clearly the distortions which satirists can perpetrate to achieve satirical effects. This is because the legal texts which he uses as a 'touchstone' themselves have a less ambiguous nature and clearer function than other, 'literary', texts invoked for a similar purpose elsewhere in this volume. Cloud shows that satirists can be both inaccurate and anachronistic and can even produce a fantastic compound of two social institutions or situations if the satiric effect demands it.

Hudson uses a wealth of material—archaeological remains, the Roman cook-book of Apicius and didactic treatises on farming and medicine—to suggest how limited are the pictures of both the rural and the urban diet in Roman Satire. She suggests that the value of food in satire is primarily moral and ideological and that certain foods bear simplified, emblematic messages which are derived from the literary heritage. Food is used to condemn certain 'types', e.g. the glutton, the gourmand and the pretentious host, and to idealise rustic existence, with little or no reflection of 'real life'. In both respects Roman Satire mirrors its producers and audience—an urban elite seeking to reinforce its own value-system.

Early in his 'femmenist' essay on the engenderment of Roman Satire Henderson asserts the importance of examining the rhetorical role and function of every detail in its context, of understanding the rhetorical target of the composition as a whole in order to see whose interests it promotes and of considering the way in which Roman culture constructed norms, ideals and fantasies. He then suggests that we cannot take anything for granted and proceeds to expose and strip away (deconstruct) centuries of (male) assumptions about the texts of Roman Satire. In so doing he presents startling pictures of (reconstructs) the four Roman satirists and he continually questions our own assumptions about these texts. This essay, which is, appropriately, couched in dialogue form, explicitly and directly challenges the reader to examine his/her attitudes to literature and hands the initiative to the reader; hence its final position in this volume.

The historian, then, must approach satire armed with an array of questions—questions about the author and audience (who wrote this? for whom?), about the *persona* (are we alienated or charmed by it? *should* we be?), about the subject-matter (why do these topics appear and others not? are they of contemporary relevance or products of the literary heritage?), about the presentation (where do we find distortion—suppression and exaggeration—in this topic? can any other evidence from antiquity confirm or contradict?), about the function of any detail in its context (is this detail there to create an emotional impact? a rhetorical effect? to convey a moral message? to entertain?) and, ultimately, about the assumptions, both personal and cultural, with which the reader himself/herself approaches the text.

Friendship in the Satirists

Roland Mayer

Roman satire was personal poetry. The writer communicated his view of chosen aspects of the world around him. But that view is not meant to be eccentric, though it may be idealised. The view should be one which recommends itself to all right-thinking men. The satirist therefore is not an individualist or a crank. Just as he addresses himself to the like-minded (or to those who can be persuaded into becoming for a time like-minded), so in his poems he may surround himself with friends whose opinions validate his own. This validation comes not just from their numbers ('Look how many people feel as I do!'), but from their position in Roman society. Society is, on the one hand, the object of satire, but, on the other, a high-ranking portion of it sets the standard of behaviour and guarantees the satirist's moral outlook as sound. The outlook is validated not because it can be intellectually grounded, as a philosophy can, but because it is shared by the best people. The satirist therefore points to them as his models or as his associates. In life he needed his friends for all sorts of support (legal, financial, emotional); in poetry he still needs them as guarantors of the essential soundness of his position.

The need of friends to whom one can appeal is the more pressing when we recall that the Roman satirists were none of them born in Rome (although all were citizens). The city was their theme, but they were in a sense outsiders. They tended to stress their apartness in various ways. Lucilius for instance decided to stick within the equestrian class, unlike his brother who became a senator. Horace, a freedman's son, knew the risks of aspiring above his station. Persius and Juvenal (probably) were also *equites* who came from parts of Italy some way away from Rome. These various aspects of 'apartness' gave independence, but also enhanced the need for attachment to friends more socially central. Lucilius had Scipio Africanus and Laelius, Horace had Maecenas. Juvenal misses such friends in his own day (which is not to say that he was unsuccessful in securing support). Only Persius appears to be less social, and he will not therefore figure largely in this essay; yet he too has his friends to whom he appeals, as we shall see.

An account of the working of patronage and friendship in Roman society might be welcome at this point, but it would prove to be highly conjectural, at least for the Republican period. It has been said of the client in the last age of the Republic that we know only that he existed.[1] His chief function was presumably to support his patron at the polls and during political campaigns, and to swell the ranks of his retinue on important occasions (for example, at trials). What his treatment was like at the hands of his patron we cannot know. We learn (somewhat to our surprise) rather more about the workings of clientship in the early empire. One reason for this is that our literary sources—Pliny's *Letters*, Martial's *Epigrams*, and the *Satires* of Juvenal—have taken as their theme their contemporary world. Horace of course did the same, but, as we shall see, he is less interested in how dependants are treated than in how they preserve their self-respect in a subordinate place in society. The imperial evidence cannot therefore be set into any context, no contrast with earlier times can be reliably constructed. Moreover there are further considerations which make it risky to use satire or satirically pointed epigrams as evidence.[2]

One general point can be made. Roman free society was founded on *officium*, loyal service, which cut both ways. The patron supported, often financially, his client, the client did whatever was expected of him (perhaps he helped the patron to relax amid amusing company, as Horace describes the relationship of the barrister Philippus and the humble citizen, Volteius Mena in *Epist.* 1.7). It is the fancied breakdown of this basic *officium* which is so vigorously denounced by Juvenal. But we must remember that we have no way of knowing how extensively the claims of *officium* were honoured in previous generations.[3] At any rate we have notice of a curious instance of satire being used to satisfy the claims of loyalty. In his *Histories* Sallust had attacked the dead Pompey. His defence was taken up by Pompeius Lenaeus, who denounced the historian in Lucilian language. Lenaeus was Pompey's freedman and so owed him both his citizenship and his standing. The death of his patron did not cancel the debt he felt he owed him.[4] The other satirists deserve a preliminary word.

None of our four writers was a careerist; they all appear to have been content with (or in Juvenal's case resigned to) equestrian status. They were not therefore like the younger Pliny who aimed to rise as a new man through the senatorial career. The decision to stay within their own social rank had important consequences—they could afford to associate with whom they chose rather than seek out those who might advance their careers. (Sir

Ronald Syme has for example recently stressed how *un*distinguished are the bulk of Horace's friends.[5]) Independence of this sort must colour the satirists' view of their friendships; they will seem to be motivated less by advantage than by affection, the truest foundation of *amicitia*.

This might be an appropriate moment to speak of Maecenas, Horace's friend, for he too is exceptional rather than typical. He was not a senator and did not seek a traditional public career as a soldier and magistrate. If therefore the chief role of clients[6] and *amici* was support of their patron at the elections or applause when he spoke in the forum Maecenas had little need for such followers. As one who stayed (like Lucilius and Horace) within his own rank he too could have afforded the luxury of fairly independent association. (Of course he will have chosen some friends just because they could be of use to him, but that use, it may be surmised, could extend chiefly towards business or pleasure; Maecenas' use of his powerful friends like Octavian was not directed to a traditional kind of self-advancement.) Maecenas then is unusual; if he treated his friends, like Virgil and Horace, as equals rather than as clients that was only right, for they all belonged to the same class, the *equites*. The picture that Horace gives us of their relationship should not therefore be seen as a reliable guide to typical dependence on a Roman grandee.

A final general point must be mentioned before we turn to the individual satirists. It concerns point-of-view. Each satirist has his own angle of vision directed upon the social life of Rome. But like all of us they tend to find what they are looking for. It is most important to bear this in mind when assessing the attitude of Juvenal to friendship in his own day (a point I shall return to). If on the other hand Horace had wanted to show that friendship in his time was less candid or sincere or disinterested than in the time of Lucilius, say, can we doubt that he would have found it difficult to pillory arrogant treatment of humble friends by wealthy patrons?[7] As it happens, however, he chose to deal with different social issues. The satirists are to a man partial in their outlook; it is imprudent to assume they aimed to present a true perspective.

Lucilius

Attacks directed against notorious and well-placed miscreants formed the most conspicuous part of Lucilian satire. It has recently been urged by Gratwick[8] that while some of the people assailed in his verses may have been the personal enemies (*inimici*) of Scipio Aemilianus, Lucilius was not hounding them for purely political motives. Such a view receives strong support from the consideration that the first collection of poems was published, rather than handed round privately, some five or six years after the death of Aemilianus in 129 B.C., when some of the named evil-doers were themselves dead. The point of publishing the attacks so late would be to show first that they were works of literary craft, divorced from a mere ephemeral object, and secondly that the people attacked were types of vicious or foolish behaviour. The vice or folly was being attacked under the name of its representative.

But attack was not perhaps all, though the fragmentary remains make confident assertions risky. Horace helps us to see a different side of Lucilius' work and of the life presented in his satires, when he tries once again (after earlier attempts in *Sat.* 1.4 and 10) to come to terms with his model in *Sat.* 2.1. Trebatius, with whom Horace imagines himself talking about the composition of satire, urges the poet, if epic fails, to praise Caesar as just and brave; in this way sensible Lucilius had praised Scipio (*Sat.* 2.1.16–17). Now it happens that we have no other notice of such encomia, but it looks as if a more positive element appeared in the poems; it may be that Scipio, or other friends, were set up as counterweights to the objects of attack. One group embodies vices or follies, he and his friends the virtues.

That the positive element, at least in an abstract or ideal way, was present is shown by the famous eleven-line definition of *uirtus*, the longest surviving fragment of Lucilius (1196–1208W). This speaks even-handedly of both what virtue is not and what it is. One element of virtuous living is opposing evil men and manners on the one hand, and on the other defending good men and manners, setting great store by them, wishing them well and living on friendly terms with them (1204–6W; Horace recalls this very passage at *Sat.* 2.1.70 when he says that Lucilius favoured virtue alone and her friends). The lost praises of his friend Scipio may well have presented him to a wider public, especially after his death, as a model of 'virtuous' behaviour. (This seems not unreasonable when we recall how Propertius, say, uses Maecenas' life as a model for his own at 3.9.21–2.)

Let me conclude with an aspect of Lucilian satire which made a special appeal to Horace, the depiction of the easy familiarity of friends enjoying each other's company. Once again the Lucilian verses are missing but Horace preserves the scene:

> To be sure when the worthy Scipio and gently wise Laelius had retired to solitude from the crowds and stage of public life, they used to joke and roughhouse with him unreservedly, until the greens had cooked for dinner. (*Sat.* 2.1.71–4)

The charm of the vignette cannot conceal its paradigmatic status (at least it held this status for Horace, and may have for Lucilius too). These are great men, rich and powerful. But prestige is left behind in Rome. In the country (we seem to be at some estate) play is appropriate, the necessary *otium* with friends. Moreover the meal, so indicative of moral bearing, is plain vegetables (*holus*). Since Lucilius had himself attacked the new-fangled luxury of the table (1235 and 1234W),[9] the simple fare points up an example set by his friends of the style appropriate to Roman gentlemen. This is life as it should be lived, simple and companionable.

Horace

Much of what Lucilius may have had to say about his friendly relations with Scipio and Laelius we have to surmise from Horace. We cannot be sure how representative this was of his work, but it clearly meant much to Horace, all of whose poetry books attest the importance of friendship to him.[10] In the first book of satires Maecenas holds centre stage, and rightly, for he rescued Horace from those insecurities of life which beset the solitary citizen (*praesidium*, 'bastion', at *Carm.* 1.1.2 is what he metaphorically calls Maecenas). Maecenas provided more than an enhanced status by association and financial backing; his company gave Horace something to idealise. The ideal is presented towards the end of the book.

In *Sat.* 1.9 Horace is pestered by a social climber, who feigns interest in him until he asks about the real object of his attentions, Maecenas (43). Horace seizes his drift at once. Maecenas is shrewd and restricts his circle of intimates, he replies. When the pest offers to improve Horace's standing within Maecenas' circle, if he is given an introduction, Horace protests:

> Life there isn't what you fancy. No household is more undefiled or holds itself so aloof from such evil practices. I assure you, it doesn't hurt me in the least that another is richer or more learned. Each one has his own position. (*Sat.* 1.9.48–52)

This description is the core of the poem, its reason for having been written. The circle of Maecenas was unusual, and that was due to the character of its formation. Horace again describes it in *Sat.* 1.6, in which he claims to give an account of his own introduction to Maecenas. (No doubt his introduction was much as he relates, but the purpose of writing the poem is less autobiographical than moral; Horace wants us to glimpse an ideal of friendly society, which Maecenas is deemed to encourage.) Maecenas is careful to choose people who deserve his attention (*Sat.* 1.6.51) and their motive is emphatically not social climbing (*praua ambitione procul*). The men who deserve notice are not necessarily well-born, but they must be of blameless life and character (*uita et pectore puro*, *Sat.* 1.6.64). This reflects the view that friendship is only possible between good men (Cicero *De amic.* 18–19) and that it is founded on virtue (Horace glances at this philosophical issue at *Sat.* 2.6.75 where he claims that the countryfolk discuss the motives for friendship over dinner). I have said that Horace's picture is idealised. I mean by that that he leaves out elements which would disturb the balance. We do not learn from Horace that Maecenas also patronised such artists as the ballet dancer Bathyllus, whom he loved.[11]

The fifth satire of the first book shows us something of how the friendship operated. Whenever an important figure went away from Rome, either on business or vacation, he would expect to be accompanied by friends (this is illustrated in *Epist.* 1.7.75–6, where the barrister Philippus takes his new friend, Volteius Mena, into the country for the *feriae Latinae*—he expects to be amused by the townee's enthusiasm for the novelties of a rural holiday). Horace begins the account of the journey from Rome as if it were purely private, and he but travelling for amusement. Only when he reaches Anxur (26) do we learn that Maecenas is to meet him there, and some others. Their purpose is a grave one, the reconciliation of estranged friends (*auersos . . . amicos*, 29). The friends Horace so scrupulously fails to name are none other than Mark Antony and Octavian, who will also be in southern Italy. The year is 37 B.C. and attempts are being made to patch up differences between them so that Octavian can deal with Sextus Pompeius in Sicily and Antony can prosecute his eastern campaigns. Horace says nothing of this, and designedly. The point he obliquely makes is that his association with the great does not reach to meddling in affairs of state—that is not his role. The real purpose of the journey is thus no more than hinted at. Horace gives himself up to amusement and to enjoying the companionship of his friends. The note of amusement, of shared jokes is stressed at 35, 57 and 98. (Cicero had complained that when his brother Quintus or Atticus were away he lacked anyone with whom to share an unguarded joke, *Ad Att.* 1.18.1.) More telling is Horace's unreserved joy at the arrival of Plotius, Varius and Virgil (the names are linked again at *Sat.* 1.10.81, with Maecenas' sandwiched between them). As Paul Lejay observed in his commentary of 1911, the feeling behind *o qui complexus* ('Oh, what embraces . . .', 43) was absent from the description of the meeting with the men of affairs at Anxur (27–9), an ingenious indication of Horace's personal preferences. As the poet exclaims, so long as he is in his right mind (*sanus*) there is nothing he would compare to an agreeable friend (44). (Or in another context, he says that is pleasant to rave (*furere*) when a friend long-missed is restored, *Carm.* 2.7.27–8.) Equally there is shared sadness when Varius departs (93). The journey to Brundisium becomes a celebration of private faces in public places (which, Auden has said, are wiser and nicer than public faces in private places).

Horace's elevation into the company of Maecenas exposed him to envy (*Sat.* 2.1.75–8). In particular it was assumed that he had inside knowledge of affairs. This he is at pains to prove untrue. He reverts to the notion of shared journeys at *Sat.* 2.6.40–6. His sole function is to make small talk with Maecenas about the weather or the next gladiatorial bout; he cannot keep a secret. This disclaimer is set against the common assumption that Horace's intimacy with Maecenas must lead to privileged knowledge of affairs of state (*Sat.* 2.6.50–8). The journey to Brundisium made the same point more largely. What the friends share are jokes, not state secrets. In those Horace has no concern; his companionship offers something else to Maecenas, disinterested sympathy.[12]

The journey to Brundisium also showed us a society of friends. Varius and Virgil, it should be recalled, had introduced Horace to Maecenas (*Sat.* 1.6.55–6). The last satire of the first book reverts to this picture (and the way had been prepared by the description of their society given to the social climber in the previous poem). The tenth satire begins with further reflections on Horace's relation to his generic model, Lucilius; he stresses his own stylistic superiority and passes to a consideration of his ideal class of readers. Of course, not the masses (*turba*, 73), but only a handful. When their names are given, it is no surprise that we recognise them, headed at 81 by the companions on the way to Brundisium. Fuscus too is there (83), who had failed to rescue the poet from the pest—a capital joke (*Sat.* 1.9.65–6). Now some of these men were to become consuls; another, Pollio, was already a leading aristocrat, *princeps ciuitatis*. But they are not named to curry favour (*ambitione relegata*, 84);[13] candour is still expected, for these men are cultivated (*doctos*, 87) as well as friends: on both counts Horace expects an honest, but informed, opinion. Friends will provide it, because, after all, he writes only for them: 'I do not recite to any but friends, and I am forced to do that, not just anywhere or in anybody's presence' (*Sat.* 1.4.73–4). The last poem, in addition to its contribution to a stylistic debate, is also a testament of friendship.

The poems we have looked at so far picture a society of friends, whose affection was grounded on shared literary pursuits (or so we may guess). The manners of that society formed an ideal, perhaps scarcely to be attained outside the pages of literature. Horace addresses himself more realistically to how we should deal with our friends in the third satire, which contrasts leniency and rigour applied to the failings of friends. In part the theme is chosen to show that the satirist is not purely malicious. But in another sense it is an aspect of a larger moral debate which aimed to reconcile the claims of friendship and of justice. He here offers a humane doctrine of behaviour; for contrast he concludes the poem with an attack upon the inhumane rigour of Stoicism. Horace sets feeling and normal behaviour (*sensus moresque*, 97) against an intolerant system that is out of touch with reality (93–4). What makes this satire remarkable is its undiminished relevance (much that we find in Roman satire, for example attacks on luxurious dinners, or on legacy hunters, is pretty much confined to ancient society). Horace knew that the smooth running of social wheels depended on tolerance and often himself craves indulgence (e.g. *Sat.* 1.3.139–40 and 6.65–71), at least for 'middling' faults. Censoriousness will not help matters; it never has and it never will. The importance is reiterated in one of Horace's latest poems. The letter to Florus, *Epist.* 2.2, ends with a series of questions that might be used in an examination of conscience. One of them is 'Do you forgive your friends?' (*ignoscis amicis?*, 210). His own answer may be found in the epilogue to the first book of *Epistles*, where he describes himself as 'easily appeased' (*placabilis, Epist.* 1.20.25). In another passage describing such an examination of the moral life, friendship again crops up as Horace tries to conduct himself in a way that will make him agreeable to his friends (*sic dulcis amicis / occurram, Sat.* 1.4.135–6).

A detail of the third satire needs to be drawn out. Horace is focussing on forbearance among friends. This virtue is but an aspect of the pleasure which friendship ought to provide constantly. Rather than make that connection overtly Horace twice refers to friends as sweet, *dulcis* (*Sat.* 1.3.69, 139–40); in both contexts the friends are so called as they forgive slight faults. *dulcis* points to compatibility or compliance (cf. *Sat.* 1.4.135–6 quoted above, or *Epist.* 1.7.12, when, addressing Maecenas as *dulcis amice*, he wants him to permit an extended vacation from Rome). That the word was common in popular parlance is shown by the pest's addressing Horace as *dulcissime rerum* (*Sat.* 1.9.4); but such intimacy was hardly justified from one whom Horace only knew by name (*notus mihi nomine tantum*, 3).[14] Sweetness is of the essence in friendship.

After publishing his collection of *Odes* Horace again turned to the hexameter, but not in the critical mode of Lucilian satire. His next literary form was something of an innovation; at least no one before him had composed a book of verse letters, *Epistulae*. In these imaginary letters to men at all levels of Roman society, Horace continues to explore among many themes the working of friendship. Central again to the collection is the poet's relation with his patron, Maecenas. But now the issue is the tension between friendship with the great and personal independence (what a philosopher would have called *autarkeia*). The seventh letter is one document in the case (but too long to discuss here). The seventeenth and eighteenth also look at the theme from different angles. In the seventeenth Horace appears to be about to offer advice on how best to make use of grand friends. But the long opening section turns into a defence of the Roman social system of 'friendship'. So unusual to our way of thinking is such an arrangement of society that some modern readers have found the letter's doctrine repellent. Rather, it is realistic. Everyone in Rome depended on someone else. A sensible man admitted the need for subordination and degree, but he had to keep to a mean of behaviour (as Horace will stress at the opening of the next letter), neither servile nor truculent. This tactful bearing was harder to maintain than it looked: some preferred a quiet life to the struggle for improvement of status (*Epist.* 1.17.37); this was hardly consonant with *Romana uirtus*, which was always striving to better its lot.

The problem arose of knowing when to call a halt to further advance. Careerism was all very well, if prosecuted with discretion, but a man needed to know when he had enough. Again, this issue is addressed in the letters under several guises. The restless need for travel is one, and the proper use of friends is another. The eighteenth letter to Lollius is about dealing with the great, the *potens amicus* (*Epist.* 1.18.44, 86). Towards the close it speaks of the need for self-sufficiency as a counterweight to relentless self-advancement. The telling phrase is *te tibi amicum*, 'being a friend to oneself' (*Epist.* 1.18.101). Our great friends can do much for our way of life and prosperity (*uita, res*) but equanimity and contentment, the dispositions that render us friendly to ourselves, depend solely on us. Hence the need for an unshakeable spirit. Friends can do much, but after all we depend most upon ourselves, and must become our own best friends. (The notion was as old as the last sentence of Plato's *Republic*, and was echoed at *Epist.* 1.3.29 *si nobis uiuere cari (sc. uolumus)*.) Only someone who had tried the striving could honourably give it up.

A number of the *Epistles* touch upon the difficulties of friendship. In the third, for instance, written to Julius Florus, who is a member of Tiberius' company of friends (*cohors amicorum*), Horace is above all concerned to reconcile the young man to an estranged friend, Munatius. He tactfully lays no blame for the rift, attributing it to hotblooded youth or worldly inexperience (*Epist.* 1.3.33). The last line however anticipates their restored affection and joint return (too often our English translations fail to do justice to the plural, *uestrum reditum*). Horace acts as a go-between again in the ninth letter, a recommendation on behalf of Septimius to Tiberius. The poet's problem was this: Septimius expected him to act because he believed Horace was the close friend of the prince (*propioris . . . amici, Epist.* 1.9.5). For his part, however, Horace is uncertain of his standing but cannot, on the other hand, fail a good and deserving friend. The letter of recommendation, one of the most banal of epistolary duties, becomes in Horace's hands a subtle document in a delicate situation. What saves him is candour; he lays the issue in all its complexity before the prince, and leaves him to decide, both how highly he rates Horace's friendship and whether to reward a man like Septimius who is willing to push himself forward discreetly.

Another letter of recommendation hints at the value of making friends. Epistle 1.12 is written to Iccius, who administers the Sicilian estates of Agrippa. It would seem that he has been complaining of inadequate financial resources. Horace reminds him of the Roman legal principle that someone who has the use and enjoyment of property (*ususfructus*) in effect has ownership. Rather than complain about poverty, Iccius should enjoy what he has the use of (*usus, Epist.* 1.12.4). His nature and his philosophical interests combine against any need for abundant riches. But Horace perceives another lack, over and above a proper sense of how to use what is available. Iccius' philosophical interests centre on what we should call physical science (tides, the apparent movement of stars). He seems to ignore the claims of ethics, which teaches us how to live in the world and deal with each other. Horace therefore encourages another sort of *usus*, familiar companionship (this link between the two parts of the letter is easily overlooked). The imperative, *utere* (22), picks up the opening emphasis on *usus*. Iccius should 'use', i.e., make the acquaintance of, Grosphus, whom Horace recommends to his notice; Grosphus is a good man and his friendship will be cheaply bought. All that is needed on Iccius' part is a proper spirit, a willingness to 'use' what he is entitled to, whether it be Agrippa's estates or Horace's friends. Once again the poet acts as go-between, bringing people together.

A great deal more could be said about the role friendship plays in Horace's satires and letters. To do the subject full justice would also require frequent appeal to the lyric poems. Suffice it to say that Horace provides one of the most striking testaments to the operation of friendship within Roman society.

Persius

The Neronian satirist, Persius, presents many interesting aspects for study, but his attitude to friendship is not one of them. What is most remarkable about his work is its break with the tradition of regarding satire as a sort of personal poetry; a symptom of this is his commitment to Stoicism (he is the only satirist whose point of view is philosophically shaded). He speaks often as a Stoic, not as one who has assessed his experiences independently. Moreover he was converted to philosophy young. He tells us in a passage to which I shall return that he fell in with a Stoic teacher when he was about seventeen. Since he died at twenty-seven, he hadn't much time to become acquainted with the world and its ways, and his dedication to philosophy may have kept his character unimprinted by the press of experience. A further consideration is his wealth. He was born an *eques Romanus* and clearly enjoyed considerable prosperity. Now wealth facilitates all things, even (or especially) the way we treat people and are treated by others. Persius, who seems to have been unambitious socially, led a facilitated life in which friendships (it may be surmised) came easily. We know from an ancient biography of the poet that he was attached to some distinguished figures (for instance, the consular historian Servilius Nonianus and the scholarly lyric poet Caesius Bassus), but he met them as social equals or even superiors. That made a difference.

There is nonetheless a remarkable affirmation of friendship with the freedman philosopher Cornutus. The fifth (and longest) satire develops after its opening into a warm avowal of gratitude for moral salvation to his teacher (5.21–52). Persius describes how he had just entered into independent manhood and how then lay spread out before his inexperienced eyes all the life of pleasure offered by Rome. From these dangers Cornutus rescued his soul. He goes on to speak of shared studies and a simple way of life (somewhat reminiscent of Lucilius, but with the addition of philosophical discipline). Fully as interesting as this encomium itself is the response of modern critics to it. It has been called unhealthily extravagant on the one hand,[15] and on the other the lines are deemed so beautiful that much is to be forgiven the poet who wrote them.[16] (It is useful to notice such opposing assessments of classical literature: we must never forget how far we are from being able to agree among ourselves about the tone of many passages. And where we cannot reach consensus, our literary judgements may be of dubious validity.) However the tone strikes the modern reader, there can be no doubting that Persius means to be impressive and to convey his sense of the debt he owes his teacher and friend. That he borrows some elements of his avowal from Horace is not to be taken as a sign of diminished sincerity. Persius is indebted, not enslaved, to Horace, and he borrows what he reckons will most forcibly convey his own feeling. It is not how a modern artist would set to work, but given the Roman practice of imitation it is a reasonable procedure.

Juvenal

Friendship, like most other good things, is not what it once was to Juvenal's way of thinking. The satires of his first book, 1–5, especially picture the shabby treatment of dependent friends, and the word *amicus* is among the commonest in his vocabulary.[17] The theme of abused friendship is part of a larger concern, the tottering rule of *officium* in Roman society.

The opening, programmatic satire draws attention to the debasement of the old relationship between patron and client, particularly in its reduction to cash payment, the well-known *sportula* (1.95). Juvenal says this dole, which was a substitute for the meal a client might have expected as a reward for a day's attendance upon his patron, is slight (*parua*, 96) and insultingly administered. Moreover there is competition for it from high-ranking Romans and foreign freedmen; even the rich and their wives contrive to secure it (1.123–6): a grim picture of commercialised patronage corrupting the upper reaches of society. But how reliable is the picture? Two of Juvenal's contemporaries must also be called as witnesses, the younger Pliny and Martial. Pliny, himself of the senatorial aristocracy, never suggests that he distributes such a dole in his household.[18] This is rather negative evidence to be sure, but it must temper a too ready belief that the *sportula* had completely replaced older forms of *officium*. Martial, whose work spans the years from A.D. 80 to 102, often refers to the dole but in ways markedly different from Juvenal (whose poems began to be published after Martial's in the second century). He never refers to magistrates accepting it, and if they had it is hard to believe that he would fail to exploit such an incongruity (the dole was worth about six Roman pennies). Nor does he suggest that women were entitled to it, doubtless because freeborn women were not traditionally clients. The impression grows that Juvenal has created a fantasy of dependency.[19] More telling yet is Juvenal's neglect of the client's point-of-view. For him cash might prove an attraction, as we learn from several of Martial's epigrams (for example, 3.14 in which a starveling Spaniard makes for Rome with an eye on the handout). Juvenal knows that the *sportula* is important income for some clients (1.119–20), but he does not reflect, as he might have, on their venality. They appeared at numerous rich houses in order to qualify for the dole (Seneca *De breu. uitae* 14) and Domitian's reinstatement of the original meal proved ruinous and had to be abandoned (cf. Martial 3.7 and 30; the starveling Spaniard of 3.14, on learning that money was no longer offered, went back to Spain!). It may be therefore that Juvenal's indignation at the *sportula* was not generally shared. A certain kind of client would get the sort of patronage he deserved.

The real issue may be that Roman society had grown out of the language it used to describe this relationship. *amicus* is a catch-all word. It may be used even of a recent or slight acquaintance to whom we want to show a friendly inclination. Intimacy was expressed more clearly by use of *meus* with the name (so *Maecenas meus* at Horace, *Carm.* 4.11.19 and *meus . . . Caluus* at Catullus 53.3), or by *familiaris* or *necessarius* or *sodalis*.[20] As early as the Gracchi we find reference to degrees of friendship (Seneca *De benef.* 6.34). That these degrees became more clearly graded and defined by Juvenal's day is not surprising. Dependence of poorer on richer was enhanced by the size of the city, the increased wealth of some men, and the existence of a royal court where degree was created as a matter of course. Society at large, as Seneca observed in the passage referred to above, would imitate this regal etiquette. But the language of friendship remained what it had always been, and those who regarded themselves as the *amici* of a plutocrat wondered that they were not treated as they fancied the friends of the great in earlier days had been treated.

Such a golden age of social relationships was pure fantasy nonetheless. Juvenal's third satire provides a clue to follow up. In it an old friend, Umbricius, has grown fed up with many aspects of life in Rome and decided to 'emigrate'. He explains to the poet that he stays poor because he cannot demean himself by performing the jobs some undertake to support themselves (3.29–48). Friendship is often guaranteed only by guilty secrets (3.49–57). He goes on to complain that the wealthy patronise hypocritical flatterers, usually Greek. The rhetoric of his denunciation is memorable: *amicus* is intoned throughout the paragraph with embittered irony (3.87, 101, 107, 112, 121) but when he comes to refer to his own *officium* he calls it slavery (*seruitii*, 125) and styles himself not friend but client (cf. 188 also). He goes on to observe that the rich look not to a dependant's meritorious character but to his income or status. Now this is just the point at which the indictment loses force, because there is no novelty in the charge. Cicero had devoted a section of his *De officiis*, 2.69–71 to this very point, and urged that merit should be our concern when we bestow patronage, not the prosperity of the 'client'. Even Umbricius' point that a son-in-law will not be chosen who is poorer than the bride (3.160–1) is anticipated in Cicero with a saying of Themistocles. Umbricius' charge is not therefore false; far from it. But neither is it a symptom of unusual deterioration of the patron-client relationship. As Jesus Himself observed, to those who have, more shall be given.

The fifth satire too can be weighed against earlier documents. The satirist there warns one Trebius that, if he seeks to attach himself to Virro with a view to a meal now and then, he will be sorry for it, since Virro's hospitality is an insult to his dependants. Now there is no doubt that hosts did treat their lesser guests churlishly. Pliny in *Ep.* 2.6 tells of a meal he was at where the better company (of which he was one) received food superior to the humbler *amici*. Martial on the other hand complains of being given poorer fare (3.60). The special form the insult took was the service of different qualities of wine—a point to which Martial too often refers (for example, 6.11.2). Juvenal tells Trebius that he will be given inferior wine (5.24–37). Was this all a recent form of 'put-down'? By no means. The unpleasing custom of serving different wines is attested as far back as the times of the Elder Cato.[21] Juvenal later turns at 107–13 to the host Virro and admonishes him to dine civilly, though he need not rival the generosity of Seneca or Piso. Nero's reign appears then to provide models of behaviour, the likes of which Juvenal misses in his own day (a point I shall return to). But Nero's nobility were not all paradigms. That very Piso whom Juvenal cites may well have been the recipient of an anonymous panegyric.[22] Its author is clearly of humble estate and he seeks admission to Piso's circle of dependants (*clientela*) on the strength of his literary talents. Among Piso's virtues the aspirant singles out his behaviour towards his clients (the writer does not hesitate to use the word *cliens* at 119 and 134, indeed he points to its supposed derivation from the verb *colo*, 'cultivate', at 109 and 113). Piso regards them as friends (*diligis ex aequo*, 113) without distinction of high and low (117). Now such praise only has point if the behaviour is exceptional, and so our panegyrist regards it. Others, he says, are arrogant (*fastosa*, 119) and buy dependants in order to mock them (a point found at Juvenal 3.152–3 as well). Thus the sort of behaviour Juvenal deplores was noticed a good generation before. I daresay that if Augustan or Republican writers had chosen to notice such things we would have more evidence of brutal arrogance from even earlier days. The notion that manners had deteriorated because we hear more about arrogance in imperial writers is implausible. Wherever there is great wealth and display there will be flunkeys and toads; so long as the rich are human they will abuse their dependants. Senecas and Pisos are always exceptional.

In the fifth satire, however, Juvenal is refreshingly even-handed. In earlier satires the humble friends of rich patrons are undeservingly mistreated for their long service (e.g., 3.122–5). But in the fifth the would-be 'friend' Trebius is drawn not by affection but for gain (however slight and at whatever cost to his self-esteem). The poem, which concludes the first book of satires, in effect points to a complete collapse of *officium* between patron and client. Neither side is blameless: the prospective client is venal, the patron pays next to nothing for his attendance. The dinner, a symbol of shared hospitality, has become the vehicle of insult, and *conuictor*, 'fellow-diner', is a badge of shame. (The ninth satire, the last of the third book, similarly charts—and for the last time in Juvenal—the patron-client bond in its corrupt state.)

Like Persius, Juvenal does not use satire as a form of personal poetry, nor does he claim to be on the receiving end of the insults he catalogues.[23] So even poems which might at first glance seem to hinge upon friendship turn out on closer inspection to use friendship simply as an excuse for a wider disquisition. The eleventh satire to Persicus, for instance, is largely (and obviously) dealing with the luxury of the table. Of course the meal to which Juvenal seems to have invited Persicus will be modesty itself. Now were this a poem by Horace we might expect some personal touches, some note of affection to suggest communication with a real friend (his letter to Aristius Fuscus, *Epist.* 1.10, springs to mind). And Juvenal's poem has been taken as such a document of friendship.[24] But the reference at 186–9 to the wife of Persicus, whose adultery distresses him, can hardly be tactful if he is a real friend of the poet's. Most recently, therefore, Persicus is reckoned to be a lay-figure, an excuse for a disquisition on culinary luxury.[25] In a similar way the Umbricius of the third satire, the friend who is leaving Rome in disgust, strikes the modern reader as vulnerable to criticism himself.[26] This is probably due less to irony at Umbricius' expense than to Juvenal's tendency to unreflecting overstatement.

Juvenal's picture of degenerate personal relationships is so moving that it is often taken to be true and complete. Since moreover it is so different from Horace's picture, it is even supposed that times had changed, and that arrogance, so frequent a theme in his satires, was rampant as never before.[27] To make this assumption is to ignore the designed partiality of Juvenal's portrait.[28] Martial, who confirms much that Juvenal says about the mean treatment of humble dependants, also provides an antidote. The reason for this is that he is not a satirist of Juvenal's stamp, nor has he, like Juvenal, chosen to focus on a single layer of social interaction. His canvas is altogether broader and more variously peopled. In Martial's epigrams we find pretty often the praises of generous and cultivated patrons, for example, the younger Pliny (10.20)[29] or the consuls L. Stertinius Avitus, Silius Italicus, and L. Arruntius Stella (whom he calls intimately *Stella meus* at 1.7.1, 4).[30] Martial's association with these men, attested in numerous poems, shows that some grandees were ready to permit considerable intimacy with talented inferiors.[31] One would never guess this from Juvenal.

Reasons may be surmised. In his programmatic first satire, Juvenal says that his poems are produced out of resentment at what is not right (*indignatio*, 1.79). If he is to uphold this claim then his themes can only be such as will convincingly arouse a similar resentment in his audience. If our response is to be *indignatio*, we cannot expect to be given a balanced account of social relationships, such as we find in Martial (read all-in-all, not selectively). Juvenal's fine declamatory style also needs to be taken into account. It is vigorous and ardent and therefore designed to arouse *indignatio* in the reader; it is not mild or suited to inducing reflection. Now Juvenal has chosen this style rather than any other because it is appropriate to some of the abuses he chooses to denounce. His success at denunciation however must not lead us to suppose that he was a specially acute or reflective observer of his society. What he claims to see annoys him but his vision may be impaired or distorted. The choice of style is still crucial. Juvenal never substantially modified his poetic tone of voice. His extreme style cries out for extreme subjects or else it imposes its grandeur on trivialities. Is it too much to say that when he reaches the fifteenth satire and denounces an Egyptian tribe for cannibalism the strain of such a restricted stylistic range becomes apparent? That cannibalism is horrid and that Juvenal's poem well conveys a sense of horror is undeniable.[32] But for how many Romans was cannibalism a temptation or a danger? Here, I believe, the style has chased up a theme to sink its teeth into, and that is true of much else in Juvenal's satires (for example, his attack on women in the sixth satire or on homosexuals in the second and ninth). The indignant style seeks appropriate fodder, and the apparent universal collapse of that venerable *officium* which once held Roman society together is highly suitable.

Friendship in Satire

Satire began as a vehicle for the expression of personal views on a variety of topics. Friendship was never raised to the front rank of its themes, as were, say, the criticism of literature and food. But so long as satiric poems were addressed to friends of the writer or concerned the behaviour of men in society friendship was bound to intrude itself more or less prominently. But after all only Horace gives it special attention, and then most dedicatedly in his *Epistles*. His interest in how men treat each other finds expression in his most social poetry. After Horace the personal note becomes fainter (this is not meant as adverse criticism) and Persius and Juvenal write much less about their own experiences. They do not however cease to present their own point of view. Satire remains one man's voice. But friendship, in the affective sense of the word, means considerably less to them, at least as a poetic theme. Human relationships are not something they care to analyse, but to describe.

City and Country in Roman Satire

Susan H. Braund

The Romans were interested in comparing and contrasting the advantages and disadvantages of city and country life and were familiar with the terms of the debate from their school days onwards. Quintilian tells us that the debate on city versus country life was a central feature of the curriculum in the schools of declamation: in fact, he places the theme 'Is town or country life better?' first in his list of debating topics for school-boys (2.4.24). It is no surprise, then, when we look in the speeches by experts in declamation recorded by Seneca the Elder to find criticisms of city life and appeals to the country as a standard of morality.[1]

When we turn to satire, we find that city and country occur quite prominently—the city as a setting for satire and as an object of attack; the country as a retreat from city life. It immediately sounds as if satire presents two of the four aspects of the debate—the disadvantages of city life and the merits of country life.

The city as setting

Why does Roman satire use the city as a setting? Roman satire is in this respect no different from most satire, which is set in the big city: Hodgart rightly describes satire as 'an urban art'.[2] Kernan's explanation is helpful:[3]

> The scene of satire is always disorderly and crowded, packed to the very point of bursting. The deformed faces of depravity, stupidity, greed, venality, ignorance, and maliciousness group closely together for a moment, stare boldly out at us, break up, and another tight knot of figures collects, stroking full stomachs, looking vacantly into space, nervously smiling at the great, proudly displaying jewels and figures, clinking moneybags, slyly fingering new-bought fashions. The scene is equally choked with things: ostentatious buildings and statuary, chariots, sedan-chairs, clothes, books, food, horses, dildoes, luxurious

furnishings, gin bottles, wigs. Pick up any major satiric work and open it at random and the immediate effect is one of disorderly profusion . . . It is no accident that most satire is set in the city, particularly in the metropolis with a polyglot people.

This last point is important—it is the fact that Rome is not simply a city but a metropolis—a cosmospolitan place and the centre of power with its court—that makes it so eminently suitable as a setting and object for satire.

There are numerous parallels to Rome which illustrate the importance of these points. From the ancient world we might mention Alexandria, like Rome a cosmopolitan place and the seat of a court, which is the backdrop for Herodas' satirical sketches in his *Mimes* in the third century B.C. Examples from Europe include Boileau's Paris, Gogol's St.Petersburg and, most obviously, London, the setting for satirical poems by Johnson, Swift, Pope and Gay's *Trivia: The Art of Walking the Streets of London*, for scenes in Byron's *Don Juan* and in Dickens's novels. In America, Nathanael West's portrayal of Hollywood in *The Day of the Locust* fits the criteria although it is neither a metropolis nor the seat of political power, because of its intensely cosmopolitan flavour in the wide variety of people attracted to the film industry to 'pay court' to the movie moguls. We are perhaps beginning to understand why Lucilius, the founder of Roman satire, 'lashed the city', according to the later satirist Persius (*Sat.* 1.114).

If we turn to Juvenal's first Satire, we can see immediately why the city is such an appropriate setting for satire. He pictures himself standing on a street corner and watching a multitude of corrupt and despicable examples of humanity passing by:

Do you not want to fill fat notebooks at the very middle of the cross-roads when . . . ? (1.63–4)

These examples are presented in a sort of parade or catalogue, which takes up most of the poem. In a relentless bombardment, Juvenal lists the scandalous and outrageous men—and women—he sees around him in Rome: the flabby eunuch who gets married, the noble lady who disgraces herself by appearing in the spectacles of the arena, a man who started out as an Egyptian slave who is now a millionaire and a show-off, a grossly overweight lawyer, gigolos who work by night, debauchers and defrauders, a corrupt official, a man who prostitutes his wife, a wife who murders her husband, and so on and so on. And, in the metropolis of Rome, bustling with visitors and trade and business from all over the empire, this picture is, just for a moment, believable. It would be patently *unbelievable* if the setting were different—a small country town, for example, or a remote outpost of the empire, or an Italian mountain village. But if we take a step back and ask ourselves on what street in contemporary London or New York you would see such a parade of scandalous and criminal behaviour, all in one day, the answer is clear and illuminating—none. It is evident that our satirist is here using the common satiric technique of distortion—that is, distortion by suppression and omission of the ordinary, everyday and uninteresting aspects of life in the city and by exaggeration of the extraordinary, colourful and fascinating aspects of life in the city. Clearly, the great metropolis *is* the place where you *might* come across the scum of humanity in Juvenal's parade, which explains the choice of Rome as the setting for satire. But equally clearly, Juvenal has used some poetic licence here in the presentation of this scum.[4]

A second illustration of why the city makes such a good setting for satire is supplied by Juvenal's second Satire, a poem rarely read or studied. The central argument of the poem is that the homosexual practices raging in Rome will spread outwards to infect all parts of the empire. The city is not only the worst place but also corrupts the rest of the world. Twice in the poem Juvenal uses country-dwellers as a standard by which to judge the corruption of Rome. At lines 72–4 he suggests that the rustics will be shocked to see a lawyer dressed in see-through chiffon:

> Look at the clothes you wear while proposing laws and statutes to the people recently victorious and with wounds still fresh and to the mountain peasants, after they have laid down their ploughs!

At 126–7 he refers to the rustic origin of the Romans:

> O father of our city! from where has such monstrous wickedness come to the shepherds of Latium?

But the corruption goes further than that. At the close of the poem he describes how foreign young men learn effeminate habits while in Rome and take them back to the edge of the empire and beyond:

> See what international relations can do: he [an Armenian boy] had come as a hostage; here boys are turned into men. For if the boys be granted a longer stay in the city, the supply of lovers will never fail. They will cast aside their trousers, knives, bridles and whips; that's how they carry back to Artaxata the habits of the young Romans. (2.166–70)

It is fitting that at the exact centre of the poem Juvenal has placed an image of corruption spreading:[5]

> Infection has passed on this plague and will pass it on to many more, just as the

whole herd in the fields perishes through the scab of a single sheep or the mange of a single pig, and one grape acquires the taint of another grape simply from the sight of it. (2.78–81)

Whatever the truth of this allegation—and it is interesting that in Satire 3 the opposite and more common allegation is made, namely that *foreigners* are responsible for the corruption of *Roman* morals—it is clear that it suits Juvenal to present the city of Rome as the centre of corruption so that he can not only describe in graphic detail the depths of depravity found in the city but also can present as the logical conclusion of this that Rome will corrupt the rest of the empire and the world: the rot starts from the centre.

It seems as if we are dealing with broad attitudes here in which the city is condemned as corrupt and immoral and the country provides a moral standard by which to measure the corruption and immorality of the city. It is these attitudes which make the city such an appealing backdrop for the satirist.

Juvenal Satire 3: the moral values

We must now turn to Juvenal's third Satire, which is one of our central texts. Satire 3 (written around A.D. 110 or later) has often been read as an account of life in Rome as experienced by a poor Roman client. For example, Carcopino cites Juvenal along with Martial and Pliny as 'our most important sources of information' about 'Roman daily life' under Trajan.[6] Paoli draws heavily on Juvenal as evidence for 'street life' and 'Rome at night', as if he were as reliable a source as legal texts.[7] A nineteenth century scholar, Edward Walford, went still further and used Satire 3 as the basis of a reconstruction of town-life in Rome.[8] We will discuss the difficulties in using this poem as evidence for everyday life later. First, we will continue discussion of Roman attitudes to city and country which emerge from this poem.

The poem is basically a huge condemnation of life in Rome with a few brief glimpses of a very different life in the country. It is delivered by a character called Umbricius. During his condemnation of the rat-race at Rome, Umbricius sketches an existence in which people are satisfied with simple things and into which rules of etiquette and status do not intrude:

There are many parts of Italy, if we accept the truth, in which no-one wears a toga but the dead. Even when grand festival days are celebrated in the grassy theatre and the familiar farce at length returns to the stage, when the rustic baby in its mother's lap is frightened by the gaping of the whitened mask, there you will see the whole audience—stalls and populace—dressed alike, and white tunics adequate for the highest aediles as the mark of their high office. (3.171-9)

By contrast, here in Rome:

Here smart dressing is carried beyond people's means . . . here all of us live in a state of pretentious poverty . . . at Rome everything has its price. (3.180-4)

The scene of the rustic community gathered together to celebrate a holiday is designed as an antithesis to Umbricius' picture of Rome—the country is a scene of leisure and relaxation, satisfaction with moderation and freedom from competition and ambition. This is just as much an idealisation as the picture of city life is an exaggeration and a caricature.

A similar idealisation occurs later, framing the section on housing (190-231). Umbricius emphasises the pleasant aspects of country life: its safety and ideal setting on cool and wooded hills (190-2); the easy access to water and the opportunities it offers for enjoying work in the vegetable garden (223-31). And in his final words in the poem Umbricius again evokes the ideal aspects of country life:

Whenever Rome restores you to your Aquinum to refresh yourself, tear me away too from Cumae to your Helvine Ceres and Diana: I will come, in my hobnailed boots, to that cool countryside to listen to your satires, if they are not embarrassed to permit it. (318-22)

The country is here envisaged as a place of refreshment (*refici*), a cool and pleasant climate (*gelidos*), where a simple man (*caligatus*[9]) may enjoy relaxation and companionship with a friend (*satirarum . . . auditor*).

These pictures are very selective: the harsh aspects of country life, amply illustrated in other sources, are omitted by Umbricius, just as he omits the pleasant aspects of city life, also well documented in other sources. The selectivity of these pictures of country and city gives a clue about their function: they are being used for their moral value. The pictures of the countryside in Satire 3 act as a foil to city life, so that the noise and hustle and bustle and complexity of city life can be emphasised through the contrast with the simplicity and tranquillity and slow pace of life in the country.

And even the setting of Umbricius' tirade is significant here. The setting is the closest approximation the city can offer to a country setting: the valley of Egeria, with its caves and shady trees and running water and shrine closely resembles the classic setting of pastoral poetry, the so-called 'pleasant place', *locus amoenus*, which provides an ideal setting for rest and song for the shepherds of pastoral poetry, as we see in Theocritus' *Idylls* and Virgil's *Eclogues*. But this *locus amoenus* has been corrupted by the city: the caves are unnatural, the spring is paved around with exotic marble and the place is occupied by Jewish beggars. Symbolically, in this poem, this indicates the corrupting power of the city—it cannot even reproduce an idyllic piece of the countryside without allowing the artificial, the greedy and the foreign to invade.[10]

The city-country antithesis

In fact, we can draw up a set of antitheses which are embodied in and conveyed by the contrast between city and country. Life in the country is safe; life in the city dangerous (190–8). Similarly, the country is cool and pleasant (190–2); the city (implicitly) hot and unhealthy. The country provides a pleasant setting for mild physical exertion (226–9); but the city is full of obstacles for those performing duties (*officia*) (239–48). A fourth antithesis is that between the simplicity of country life and the artificiality and pretentiousness of city life, well illustrated in lines 165–83. Similarly, life in the country is cheap but life in the city expensive, as shown by the contrast of rents (223–5). Moreover, in the country the community is shown acting together (177–8) whereas city-life is marked by competition between individuals, and unfair competition at that (e.g. from Greeks and other upstarts). A further antithesis is that Rome is occupied by the rich and by foreigners, forcing poor Romans to retreat to the countryside (e.g. 162–3). And finally the city is full of people and things, as the entire poem shows, whereas the country is empty (*uacuis . . . Cumis* 2). All these antitheses add up to an attitude which identifies city life with greed, corruption and selfishness and idealises country life as a haven where a better set of moral values can be found.

So far, we have argued that the treatment of city and country in Roman satire reveals much about the moral values of the Romans: those of which the Romans approved are set in the country and those of which they disapproved are set in the city. But if we try to use Satire 3 as a source for details of everyday life, there are considerable problems. We must now indicate some of the difficulties and limitations.

Umbricius: significance and symbol

The first difficulty is that the person who delivers the condemnation of Rome in Satire 3 is not 'Juvenal',[11] the voice we hear in the other satires, but Umbricius. This very fact should ring some warning-bells. *Why* does Juvenal choose not to deliver this tirade in the first person? Does it mean that he wishes to distance himself from the views expressed? This seems to be confirmed by the fact that at the end of the poem his friend Umbricius leaves Rome in disgust but 'Juvenal' stays behind. Perhaps Rome is not so disgusting, after all ... The distinction introduced gives a perspective to the condemnation of Rome in the poem.

Another question we might now ask is, who is this Umbricius who delivers the attack on Rome? One answer is very straightforward—that Umbricius was a real person, a friend of Juvenal in real life who really left Rome in disgust. There is no way of proving or disproving this. It is true that the name Umbricius was a real name, though rare.[12] But on the other hand it is also true that the names which are used in Roman satire, as in all satire, are very often chosen for their symbolic significance. Names such as Ofellus, 'Mr Cutlet', Porcius, 'Hog' and Cupiennius, 'Randy' seem to be chosen by Horace to suit their contexts in the Satires purely or chiefly because of their derivations.[13] Similarly, Petronius in his prose satire-cum-novel, *Satyrica*, seems to have chosen names for his characters which are significant and suitable: Encolpius, 'Embraced', and Giton, 'Neighbour'.[14] And the name Umbricius works well on a symbolic level. It makes us think of the Latin word *umbra*, which means 'shadow' or 'ghost'. If we apply this meaning to Umbricius in Satire 3, it suggests that he is a ghost, departing, appropriately enough, at sunset (3.316), his destination, appropriately enough, Cumae—the mythical entrance to the Underworld, according to Virgil *Aeneid* 6 (106–7). And why is he departing from Rome? He is departing in disgust from a Rome which has become un-Roman (*Graecam Vrbem* 3.61), because he sees himself as a paragon of Roman virtue: unlike his contemporaries he cannot lie or commit murder or act as an adulterer's go-between or be an accomplice in theft (3.41–8). Yet to survive in Rome, these are precisely the 'skills' you need. That is why he can stay no longer. And unlike those who are successful in Rome, he is truly Roman, born on the Aventine (84–5). Moreover, he longs for the good old days when, for example, one prison was enough for Rome (lines 312–14), and thus Juvenal characterises him in such a way as to introduce into the poem a past-present antithesis which serves the same function as the country-city contrast: both condemn modern Rome for its corruption through contrast with a perfect, idealised opposite. And like the city-country antithesis, this past-present antithesis conveyed by Umbricius reveals more about Roman attitudes than about conditions in Rome of the imperial age or Rome of the early Republic. Further, if we regard

Umbricius as the spirit of Roman-ness, fleeing an un-Roman Rome, he resembles (in satiric form) the virgin goddess of myth, who flees from the world, horrified by man's wickedness.[15] But instead of fleeing to heaven, as the virgin goddess of myth does, Umbricius flees to the gates of the Underworld.[16] Apparently Juvenal has chosen the name Umbricius so that his *fictional* character can convey a *symbolic* message, that modern Rome is so corrupt and un-Roman that the ghost of Roman-ness has to leave.

Although Umbricius evidently sees himself as a morally commendable upholder of old-fashioned values, this does not necessarily make his comments reliable. In fact, his chief reason for leaving seems to be his jealousy of those who have succeeded and anger towards them. His jealousy he reveals throughout his tirade in his self-presentation and the objects of attack; his anger he reveals both in his resentful tone and in the sheer length of his tirade. The effect is to detract somewhat from the high moral position he claims;[17] and his anger and jealousy must in turn affect the reliability of his picture of Rome.

The linguistic signs of anger[18] are present in Umbricius' speech in abundance, for example, angry questions (38–40, 49–50, 61, 81–5—three, 126–30); angry exclamations (e.g. 66); vocabulary of not enduring (60, 152 *durius*); and sweeping generalisations (*nullus, nulla* 22, *omnia* 77, *nihil* 109, *nusquam* 125, *omnes* and *omnia* 182, *nemo* 211 twice, *undique* 247, *tot . . . quot* = 'every' 274, *omnes* 308, *maximus* 310). A further sign of anger is that Umbricius gets totally carried away in his condemnation of Rome, so that we might fairly conclude that he is a little unbalanced. The poem quite clearly starts as a quiet and sad conversation between two friends, 'Juvenal' and Umbricius, who meet to say farewell. 'Juvenal' has come to see Umbricius off and Umbricius takes the opportunity to explain his reasons for leaving Rome:

> While all his goods were loaded on to a single waggon, Umbricius halted by the old dripping arches of the Porta Capena . . . From here we went down into Valley of Egeria with its artificial grottoes . . . Here Umbricius began . . . (3.10–21)

So far so good. But does 'Juvenal' get a chance to offer any consolation or encouragement to his departing friend? No. Soon, caught up in the vehemence of his condemnation of Rome, Umbricius seems to forget where he is and begins addressing the Romans at large, as if he were proclaiming or preaching to them from a public platform. The crucial indication of this comes at line 60 where he says:

> Citizens of Rome, I cannot stand a Greek Rome.

In fact, his choice of words reveals that he imagines himself in exactly the right place for appealing to the public at large against injustices suffered. His exclamation 'O citizens of Rome' (*Quirites*) is exactly how a speaker would address his audience when appealing to them at a public meeting (*contio*).[19]

And the rest of his tirade sounds more like a public declamation than the private conversation it supposedly is. Only at the very end of the poem, as the sun moves round and his driver signals him does he return to the original setting of the poem and address his friend (3.315–22). But for the intervening 300 lines, he has been totally engrossed, even obsessed, with his theme. This leads us to doubt the balance of his mind—and to doubt the reality of his vividly drawn picture of the corruption of Roman life.

As well as betraying his anger, his words also betray his jealousy. The first topic of his speech is his criticism of rich upstarts—the men born in the gutter who have made a fortune by charging high fees for the jobs no one else wanted to do, such as dredging the rivers, clearing the sewers and conveying the dead to burial (3.30–40). Clearly, Umbricius would not consider tackling such jobs himself—but he seems to be jealous of the money made from such activities. The same goes for his second topic —foreigners (58–125). Again, he regards these Greeks and other Easterners as impostors, who have taken the place of trusty Roman clients like himself:

> There is no place for any Roman here, where some Protogenes or Diphilus or Hermarchus rules, whose national fault is never to share a great friend but to monopolise him. For when he has dropped into his friend's ready ear a little of his natural and national poison, I am removed from the doorstep: my long years of servitude are gone for nothing; nowhere is it so easy to jettison a client. (3.119–25)

He is envious of the money and success the Greeks win for themselves by their flattery. But he really betrays himself when he admits that he cannot compete with them—in a way which suggests that if he could, he *would*!:

> We too can offer these same compliments, but it is they who are believed. (3.92–3)

He proceeds to a more general condemnation of the rat-race at Rome (126–89); the fact that everyone is judged by the amount of money he has is particularly annoying to him:

> each man's trustworthiness is measured by the size of his bank balance. (3.143–4)

It seems clear, however, that he would not say this if he were rich! In fact, if we read the poem attentively, we notice a gap between Umbricius' presentation of himself and his revelation of his situation. Umbricius presents himself as a failed client (e.g. 125), who has been ousted from his rightful position by those more clever and adaptable than he. He is not rich—which helps to explain his envy of the rich. But—it is important to observe—he is not incredibly poor either. True, he is not rich enough to be able to afford a house in both town and country (as the well-off at Rome were), but it seems reasonable to presume that he has arranged accommodation at Cumae. He is neither as poor as Cordus (203–7) nor as rich as Persicus (220–2) but has one waggon-load of possessions. He talks as if he has more than one slave (166–7). His central complaint is that he cannot keep up with the expected standard of living in Rome (168 and 182–3). His viewpoint, therefore, is not of someone at the bottom of society but simply of someone who would like to be better off! So he reveals that, although he now condemns the rat-race at Rome, he has up to now has been participating in it. This suggests a double standard and detracts a little from the dignity of his stance. For all these reasons, it becomes hard to take his picture of Rome entirely seriously.

Everyday life in Rome?

Juvenal maintains his characterisation of Umbricius as a jealous failure throughout the poem. We have already seen that in the early parts of Umbricius' tirade, this is manifested in his attacks on the rich and successful. The contrast he draws there between rich and poor is the central feature of the second part of the poem too—the part of the poem which appears to offer the most information about life in Rome (190–308).

The first topic here is the frequent collapses and fires which destroy city dwellings (190–231). Of the collapses of buildings Carcopino says 'the satirist has not exaggerated' and he goes on to say, 'Dread of fire was such an obsession among rich and poor alike that Juvenal was prepared to quit Rome to escape it: "No, no, I must live where there is no fire and the night is free from alarms!" He had hardly overstated the case'.[20] Carcopino seems to regard Satire 3 as simple description. But is this the evidence it might appear to be?

It is certainly true that fires did rage and buildings did collapse in Rome. Back in the late Republic, Cicero writes to his friend Atticus of the collapse of some of his tenement houses (*Ad Att.* 14.9.1). Crassus is said by Plutarch to have taken financial advantage of collapse and conflagration (*Crass.* 2.4). Nearer to Juvenal's own time, Seneca mentions in passing 'tenement walls crumbled and cracked and out of line' (*Ira* 3.35.5). And a contemporary of Juvenal, Aulus Gellius, reports someone saying that if a remedy could be found to prevent houses in Rome from catching fire so often, he would sell his country property and buy in the city (Gell. 15.1.2–4). The two complaints in fact seem to occur together as part of the stock worries of the well-off, for example at Catullus 23.9 and at Propertius 2.27.9. Moreover, the worries expressed by the writer on architecture, Vitruvius, (e.g. *Arch.* 2.8.20), along with the legislation enacted by various emperors (Nero: Tacitus *Ann.* 15.43, Trajan: Aurelius Victor *Epitom.* 13.13— maximum height 60 feet) suggests that tenement buildings (*insulae*) were particularly likely to catch fire, because the walls of their upper stories were constructed of wooden partitions which burned very easily, the foundations being too insecure to bear the weight of brick walls.

Clearly, collapses and conflagrations did occur. But this section of Juvenal 3 is not a documentary about the living conditions of the urban plebs in Rome but part of Umbricius' complaint against Rome. This explains the contrast here between the situations of the poor man and the rich man when their accommodation burns down: the poor man, who has nothing, is rendered totally destitute, but the rich man receives so many gifts and so much money from sympathetic friends that he is richer than he was before the fire![21] This fits exactly with Umbricius' earlier complaint, that at Rome you need to be rich to be taken seriously (143–4). It is natural that the satirist will choose details which emphasise the gulf between rich and poor, the extreme cases of a very poor man and a very rich man, in order to strengthen Umbricius' condemnation of life in Rome. Similarly, when Umbricius declares that for the annual rent of a city garret[22] you could buy an estate in the country, we cannot treat this as evidence, as Carcopino does,[23] for either rents in Rome or the price of estates in the country. It is not reliable evidence because, even if the amounts are credible (and other evidence from a different kind of source would be needed to confirm this), they are likely to be selected from the extreme top of the scale in the case of the city rent and the extreme bottom of the scale in the case of the country estate, or possibly even rounded further up and down, to reinforce the contrast. Again, this item must be considered in its context, namely, as part of both the rich-poor antithesis and the city-country antithesis which Umbricius is drawing.

The next section (232–308) features scenes on the streets of Rome: here Juvenal continues to use the contrast between rich and poor as the backbone of Umbricius' complaint; and this must continue to affect our view of the reliability of the material as evidence about life in Rome. Again, it is likely that Juvenal has chosen extreme examples, to reinforce his characterisation of Umbricius as a jealous failure. So he contrasts the insomnia of the poor man with the rich man's sound sleep in the sweeping statement, 'You need to be rich to sleep in the city' (235). The poor man evidently inhabits a room overlooking the street but the rich man is far removed from the noise in a room at the rear of his substantial town house. Again he contrasts the rich man's ease of travel in his comfortable litter with the poor man's struggle on foot (239–48). And he observes that the drunken thug is not so foolish as to attack a rich man's retinue but waits for a poor man who walks home unattended (282–8).

There is besides the rich-poor contrast another principle of structure visible in this section. The scenes are arranged in a chronological sequence. We start with the insomnia of the poor man caused by the night-time traffic (232–8). Then in the morning, when duty calls (*si uocat officium* 239—most likely the *salutatio*, the morning greeting-call paid to the patron), the poor man has to suffer the hustle and bustle and dirt of the street (239–48). Later in the day, he may even suffer a fatal accident while returning home (254–67). If he ventures out in the evening there are perils such as falling pots and slops (268–77). And on his return home he may meet a drunken thug itching for a fight (278–301). Even when he is 'safely' indoors, he may meet a burglar or murderer (302–8). What Juvenal has done here is to cram into a fictitious 24 hour period all the horrors which a poor man could conceivably meet on the streets of Rome, though *not* conceivably within 24 hours. In no way is this to be read as a documentary account. Rather, the satiric techniques of selection—of the most entertaining and telling incidents—and of compression—their presentation as happening within one 24 hour period—are in full view.Both the selection of details to enhance the rich-poor contrast and the satiric compression here limit the reliability and usefulness of this passage as evidence for life in Rome.

Entertaining the intellectuals: parody shapes 'reality'

Creating a satirically exaggerated criticism of life in Rome and a faintly humorous character to deliver this criticism may be Juvenal's chief concerns in this poem—but they are not his only ones. He is also interested in entertaining a highly educated audience with wit and literary allusions and parody. Of course, wit and literary allusions and parody do not necessarily detract from the reliability of evidence—but they do suggest that details are chosen primarily on the basis of what they offer in terms of intellectual entertainment.

For example, the description of the obstacles to the poor man's progress through the street (3.243–6) makes it sound like a battle, a mock-epic battle. It is apparent that Juvenal has chosen details which lend themselves to a mock-epic treatment.[24] The death in a traffic accident which follows, itself hardly ordinary, is presented as a travesty of the descent of the epic hero into Hades. For example, the mention of the muddy whirlpool recalls an earlier travesty of a (supposed) hero's descent into Hades—that of Dionysus in Aristophanes' *Frogs*, in which Dionysus is warned that he will find 'masses of mud and ever-flowing sewage' in the Underworld (*Frogs* 145–6). Moreover, the phrase 'muddy whirlpool', *caenosi gurgitis*, with the rare adjective *caenosi*, 'muddy', describing the Styx, seems to be chosen deliberately to echo Virgil's description of Acheron, *turbidus hic caeno . . . gurges*, 'the whirlpool thick with mud' (*Aen.* 6.296). There is another echo of Virgil in the new corpse's reaction to the sight of Charon the ferryman, to shudder: *horret | porthmea* 265–6, cf. *portitor horrendus Aen.* 6.298.[25] Echoes like these reinforce the epic potential of this scene. That potential is not, however, realised, thanks to details such as calling the new corpse *nouicius*, a word which literally denotes 'a newly-imported slave' and so means here 'a newcomer', hardly a glamorous way to portray a mythological scene.[26] Similarly, Juvenal provides a bathetic equivalent to Virgil's explanation of why the shades cannot be transported across the river. In both authors it is, in effect, because the shades have received no proper burial; but Virgil expresses this majestically whereas Juvenal trivialises it by reference to the coin placed in the mouth of the corpse (or, rather, to its absence). And in another author and another context, the contrast of the household busy in blissful ignorance preparing dinner while its master is sitting by the Styx might arouse pathos, but here Juvenal guarantees a mock-epic effect with the mundane and unpoetical list of the household's activities (lines 261–3: washing the dishes, lighting the fire and preparing strigils, towels and oil-flask)

In the next lines, the intellectual entertainment is provided primarily by two puns in the Latin. The first is on *testa* (a tile; line 270) and *intestatus* (an adjective describing someone who has not made a will; line 274); the second is in the phrase *subiti casus inprouidus*, where *casus* is used in two senses, 'fall' and 'accident': 'unwary of sudden accident | fall[ing pot]'. The presence of puns does not detract from the fact that the hazard of falling objects was a real and serious problem.[27] It does however invite a more detached and light-hearted view of such situations. Modern comedy sometimes uses people being struck on the head by falling objects as a source of humour. That this might be humorous to the Romans too is suggested by Plautus *Amphitruo* 1034 where Mercury apparently while standing on the roof throws water on to Amphitryon below.[28]

More elevated literary overtones return as the pedestrian encounters a thug. The drunken thug is itching for a fight, as restless as Achilles in the *Iliad*, who after the death of his friend Patroclus spends all night tossing and turning (*Iliad* 24.10–11). This is another case of mock-epic and exaggeration: the epic 'parallel' serves to emphasise the sordidness of the situation—because the thug is so utterly unheroic, so very different from the great Achilles, and the sordid details are exaggerated until the thug is larger than life.[29] At the end of the section, a tone more reminiscent of Roman comedy is injected, when with heavy irony, Umbricius describes it as 'the poor man's freedom', *libertas pauperis haec est*, to return home with a few teeth in his head (299–301):[30] injury has been added to insult (292–6).

As a final signal that we should not take this picture of life in the buildings and on the streets of Rome entirely seriously, Juvenal puts into Umbricius' mouth an exaggerated version of a cliché (309–11). The cliché is that in time of war ploughshares and other agricultural implements are melted down and made into swords. Juvenal alters this so that Umbricius says that nowadays there are so many criminals that ploughshares and so on are melted down to make fetters and chains. We recognise the cliché. We recognise the alteration. We recognise the satiric exaggeration. The exaggeration is typical of Umbricius' pessimistic view of modern Rome. And, finally, in the nostalgic contrast between the crime-free past and the criminalised present, we also recognise another moral contrast which reveals more about Roman attitudes than Roman life.

The literary tradition

Another factor besides the aim to provide intellectual entertainment which limits the reliability of Satire 3 as evidence is the influence of the literary tradition in which Juvenal was working. Roman literature, perhaps much more than modern literature, was heavily influenced by tradition. A Roman poet was expected to acknowledge his eminent predecessor(s) in his chosen genre by generally handling the same themes, and, for example, imitating particular passages. So Juvenal will have been aware of and influenced by portrayals of city life by his satiric predecessors, Lucilius, the founder of the genre, and Horace. And in fact, when we set alongside one another the descriptions of city life in all three poets, a considerable overlap can be seen, especially in the selection of details, despite the long time-scale involved. Therefore we cannot rule out the possibility that the tirade put into Umbricius' mouth in Satire 3 derives as much from literary tradition as it does from real life in second century A.D. Rome.

So, for example, look at a fragment of Lucilius, writing in the second century B.C., on life in Rome (1145–1151W):

> But as it is, from morning till night, on holiday and workday, all the people and all the senators alike bustle about in the Forum and nowhere leave it; all dedicate themselves to one and the same interest and skill—to be able to swindle with impunity, to fight cunningly, to strive using soft words as weapons, to act the 'fine fellow', to lay ambushes, as though all of them were enemies of all men.

Comparison of this with Juvenal 3 reveals that both authors criticise urban life for its bustle, competitiveness, cheating and crimes. Similarly, there are a number of correspondences between Juvenal 3 and Horace's portrayal of city life in *Epistles* 2.2.65–76:

> how can you ask me to turn out poetry in Rome, with so many worries and so many onerous duties? One man wants me to act as a sponsor, another to drop all my engagements and hear his work; this one is poorly on the Quirinal, that one across the Aventine; both expect a visit. (Note how conveniently close they are!) 'The streets,' you say, 'are clear; there's nothing to block your inspiration.' A feverish builder charges past with his mules and workmen; a huge contraption heaves a beam and then a boulder; wailing funerals smash their way through lumbering wagons. There goes a mad dog; here's a muddy pig. Try composing tuneful lines in the middle of that!

Both Horace and Juvenal mention the duties of city life, including attending literary recitations, and the chaos on the streets caused by builders' waggons and mud, and these points of similarity are reinforced by a number of verbal echoes.[31] These overlaps seem to be too close and too numerous to be coincidental: it looks as if Juvenal deliberately echoes his predecessors' treatment of the theme, just as many of Horace's details may in turn be drawn from this passage or lost parts of Lucilius. That is, the literary tradition has influenced his choice and handling of material. This is not to say, of course, that none of these details is drawn from real life; but the realisation that certain details may be included and others excluded under the influence of the literary tradition must affect our use of such details as evidence for everyday life.

What is more, these passages from Lucilius and Horace can no more be used as evidence for life in Rome during the second century B.C. or late first century B.C. than can Juvenal's picture of Rome in the second century A.D. Each of these passages has its context within which it serves a purpose. That of the passage from Lucilius is unfortunately lost to us, although a hint of it is provided by the author who has preserved this fragment by quoting it. In introducing it Lactantius calls it Lucilius' description of 'that dark way of life,' *tenebrosam istam uitam*.[32] This makes it sound as if its original context was similar to that of Juvenal 3, especially given that Juvenal seems to dwell on the 'shady' side of life, life in garrets (*tenebras* 225) and on dark and seedy streets. The context of the passage from Hor. *Epistles* 2.2 we *can* assess, and it is very different from Juvenal 3. Horace wheels out a standard picture of the inconveniences of city life as an explanation of why he cannot write poetry in Rome (lines 65–86) and proceeds to evoke briefly the standard idyllic picture of the country as an ideal setting for composing poetry (lines 77–8). This explains the emphasis on noise and bustle in his portrayal of city life. His presentation of both parts of the city/country antithesis functions on the same level as other items which he weaves into his satirical poems to augment his argument, such as fables and parables and caricatures, and cannot be read as a straightforward description.

In fact, it is noticeable that portrayals of city life hardly seem to vary through the relatively long time span covered by Roman satire—between Lucilius and Juvenal is more than two centuries. A historian might look to a source like Roman satire to provide evidence for change. But it is hard to find any here. The Greeks and other Easterners condemned by Juvenal, writing in the second century A.D., are present too in second century B.C. Lucilius;[33] and the Spaniards and Africans we might expect to feature in a picture of second century A.D. Rome are nowhere to be found in Juvenal. This may very well be explained by the strength of the influence of the literary tradition.

Another thing a historian might expect to find in Juvenal is a reflection of contemporary life. But in fact, Juvenal is notoriously elusive on this point—which probably explains why scholars have located him at various dates in the late first century A.D. and early second century A.D. Working from the few references or allusions to recent and contemporary events and literature, Syme quite rightly places Juvenal in the second and third decades of the second century A.D.[34] That is, he was writing during the period 110–130 A.D., under the emperors Trajan (98–117 A.D.) and Hadrian (117–138 A.D.). But what do we learn of life in Trajanic and Hadrianic Rome? Very little. It has been pointed out that the world of Juvenal's *Satires* is very much that of the late first century A.D., the world of Nero and the Flavian emperors, especially Domitian. This in turn has been explained by reference to the literature produced by Juvenal's contemporaries and immediate predecessors. When Juvenal was writing

Book I (Satires 1–5), Tacitus was writing his *Histories*; soon he would move on to his *Annals*, and soon Suetonius would be at work on his biographies of the emperors from Caesar to Domitian. The trend among intellectual circles was backward-looking. Moreover, writers like Juvenal would have been familiar with the works of Statius and Martial and Pliny, which, in their different ways, provided pictures of life in Rome, at court and in the provinces under Domitian in particular. It is not therefore surprising that the pages of Juvenal are full of parallels with these authors, details from them and allusions to them—parallels, details and allusions which give Juvenal's Satires a very Domitianic flavour and which would have been recognised by Juvenal's audience.[35] The influence of recent and contemporary literature then is yet another impediment to reading Juvenal as straightforward evidence for life in Rome.

Satire 3 as evidence: attitudes not facts

That concludes our examination of Juvenal 3. Some of the difficulties and limitations in using the poem as a document about Roman social life in the second century A.D. have been indicated. The choice of the genre of satire—and with it the influence of the literary tradition on the choice of details, the presentation of an angry character, the effects of satirical techniques such as distortion, exaggeration, compression and omission, the desire to entertain through wit and humour—has its effect on the presentation of life in the metropolis. If we seek to use details as evidence, we must always examine what purpose the detail is serving in its satirical context and we must always seek corroboration of the detail from other sources, other sources with no satirical axe to grind. What the poem does reveal is Roman attitudes, attitudes to both city and country: a pessimistic and critical view of the city, which attributes to it faults such as greed, and an idealistic view of the country, which is where true Roman morals and values, especially those associated with the past, are located.

Horace Satires 2.6: the superiority of country life.

A very similar picture emerges from the second of our central texts, Horace Satires 2.6 (written in 30 B.C.) which, like Juvenal's third Satire, ends with one character saying farewell to another. The contrast between city and country is the backbone of the poem. Horace explores the theme both in his own person and in the fable of the town mouse and the country mouse with which the poem ends. According to 'Horace', life in the city is busy and hurried, marked by ambition and greed and triviality and superficiality. Instead he longs for life in his country retreat, the Sabine farm given to him by his patron. For him, life in the country is calm and slow, a life of contentment and satisfaction and depth and sincerity. The fable of the mice illustrates the same points. The country mouse enjoys a frugal and safe existence. The town mouse, by contrast, lives a life of luxury and danger. As with Juvenal 3, a set of antitheses emerges in the contrast between city and country. Firstly, Horace, speaking in the first person (1–76), sets up oppositions between the duties and business of city life and the freedom and calmness of country life; between the fast pace of city life and the slow pace of country life; between the amibiton and greed found in the city and the contentment and satisfaction achieved in the country; and city life is portrayed as superficial whereas country life is profound and therefore real.

Secondly, the fable (77–117) reveals oppositions between luxurious and frugal food, easy life and hard life, safety and danger and independence vs. dependence. The moral superiority of country life to city life again emerges clearly from these antitheses. Let us consider the picture of country life first. In the opening lines of the poem, Horace describes his farm literally as a place which will make him self-sufficient. Symbolically, his farm represents his independence from the rat-race of Rome and its duties and obligations:

> Well then, now that I've left town for my castle in the hills what can I better celebrate in the satires of my lowland muse? Here I'm away from the status struggle . . . (2.6.16–18).

His farm is clearly a 'castle in the hills' not literally but symbolically: it is his stronghold and refuge.[36] In lines 59–76 the country provides an opportunity to relax and read widely; moreover, it provides a setting for wonderful dinners with friends at which the menu is simple, people partake of drink as they please instead of according to convention and the conversation is on topics which *really* matter, such as the meaning of life (*summum bonum*), instead of the gossip of city dinner-parties. Essentially, the country life is presented as a backdrop for the enjoyment of philsophy (the 'writers of old', line 61) and leisure (*otium*) and, above all, true friendship. Turning to the fable which Horace adapts from Aesop, we see from lines 79–89 and the last two lines of the poem that the country mouse enjoys simple fare and that his lifestyle is independent and safe.[37]

These two pictures complement one another to create an idealistic picture of country life, not so much in the soft primitive sense of the spontaneous fertility of Nature (though there is a hint of this at the beginning in Horace's description of his farm)[38] but more in the hard primitive sense of satisfaction with a moderate life-style which goes hand in hand with proper moral standards. The country is a place where simple moral values assert themselves. In Horace's case this is manifested in his freedom from silly etiquette and in the possibility of enjoying true leisure and friendship and being truly independent. In the case of the mouse, this is manifested in his frugal life which brings its own reward in the opportunity for relaxation and sincere hospitality on a special occasion; from his trip to the city he learns to be content with his independent (and modest) life-style.[39]

This idealisation of the country in which proper forms of leisure are enjoyed as a reward for hard work and moderation we meet elsewhere in Roman literature—for example, in Horace's earlier poem, *Epode* 2, in Lucretius 2.20–36 and most obviously in Virgil's *Georgics*, almost exactly contemporary with Horace's second Book of Satires.[40] Moralists and historians also praise the country life, often in the context of an analysis of the moral decline of Rome from the 'good old days' when the tough rustic existence created tough robust leaders,[41] an attitude to the countryside instilled in all Roman writers from an early age in the schools of declamation (as we noticed above).

Horace on city life

We have established that Horace's idealistic presentation of life in the country belongs to the Roman ideology whereby the country is morally superior to the city. Is the same true of his portrayal of city life? Lines 23–59 of Satire 2.6 describe the jobs which must be undertaken by Horace during the morning. The function of this section within the poem as a whole is to present the antithesis to the leisure or *otium* of country life, that is, the *neg-otium* (work, business, trouble) of city life. Within this framework, Horace has chosen to present the cliché of the *negotium* of city life in a highly personalised way, which makes it more difficult to use the poem as evidence for Roman social life. What he describes is not simply the general hustle and bustle of city life (rather as he does later at *Epist.* 2.2.65–75 quoted above) but the burdens he bears because of his position in society, a position of potential privilege and influence because of his relationship with Maecenas. He sketches tasks and duties which might arise in a morning—to act as Maecenas' representative, to attend business meetings and to get Maecenas' signature on a document (23–39). While all these activities are perfectly plausible, they are not the activities of just any official in Rome but of a member of the ruling elite. Moreover, we might note the role of selection and presentation here. Horace has chosen some of the less attractive aspects of city life and omitted, for example, the cultural dimension, which was considerable, especially in the circles in which he moved, which included Virgil and other literary men (just consider, for example, the list at the end of *Sat.* 1.10, in lines 81–8). And even when he does mention more pleasant occasions, such as being asked to accompany Maecenas to the games or exercise in the Campus Martius (48–9), he does so in order to condemn the jealousy and curiosity this arouses in others (49–58). That is, he shapes his material to make a moral point: 'That's how the day is wasted. In exasperation I murmur: "When shall I see that place in the country . . . ?" ' (59–60).

The moral attitude implied by the city mouse in the fable is more straightforward. He is cast as a hedonist[42] who turns his nose up at the rustic food served up to him by his country friend and prefers the luxuries available from a rich man's table in the city, luxuries which are lavishly described in lines 102–5. But this luxurious life-style is one of utter dependency—the city mouse is a 'parasite', feeding from the table of another. What is more, his life-style is fraught with danger, here in the form of the dogs who burst in. Why is it the dogs who pose the danger to the city mouse and not the rich man himself? Partly because this is an animal fable, but partly because the dogs too are dependent on the rich man. Horace is indicating the fierce competition between the rich man's dependents or parasites, a competition which the country mouse does not experience, of course, in his independent and solitary existence in the country.

What we have here is a stereotyped picture of city life—a life which may bring luxury but also brings complexity, duties, dependence and even danger. The picture reveals more about Roman attitudes to city life than it does about city life itself.

Is the city so very bad?

Taking these two pictures—of city and of country—together, we cannot deduce that everyone at Rome wanted to leave the perils and duties of city life for country simplicity. In fact, the *implicit* message of the poem contradicts any conclusion we might draw about Horace's desire to leave the city. Horace betrays his obvious enjoyment of the importance his association with Maecenas brings, e.g. 32 'I like that, I admit, and it's sweet music in my ears', particularly in his selection of duties which draw attention to his 'intimacy' with the great man rather than less interesting duties. This implicit message serves the same function as the distinction which Juvenal draws between his first person speaker or *persona*, who utters the first 20 lines of Satire 3, and Umbricius, whose tirade against Rome makes up the rest of the poem. Juvenal had no need to draw this distinction and must have done so for a purpose. Through this distinction he gives a perspective to Umbricius' complaint: for every Roman who leaves the metropolis in disgust, there is another who, while agreeing with the deplorable aspects of city life, is perfectly content to remain in the city. That is why the first 20 lines of the poem, spoken in the first person, provide a preview (though in a rather humorous vein) of the themes which Umbricius will develop in his speech; and that is why our attention is drawn, at the end of the poem (lines 315–22), to the fact that while Umbricius is leaving, his friend is not.

Symbolic values again

We have seen that in Satire 2.6 Horace uses city and country as symbols of *negotium* and *otium* and especially as symbols of dependence and independence. Later in his satirical writings, Horace returns to the same theme, for example in *Epistles* 1.10 in which Horace contrasts himself with his city-loving friend Aristius Fuscus, and in *Epistles* 1.7, where Horace explains why he is declining Maecenas' insistent invitation to return to Rome from the country. For Horace, it is not so much the actual delights of the country which keep him there, but what the country represents symbolically for him—*otium*, true friendship[43] and freedom from excessive dependence on Maecenas:

> Small things for the small. It isn't royal Rome that attracts me now, but quiet Tibur or peaceful Tarentum. (*Epist.* 1.7.44–5; cf. *Epist.* 1.10.32–3)

Later in the same poem, Horace presents a different version of the city-country contrast. He tells a story in which a man who enjoys a modest life-style in the city is set up by his patron in a country estate which causes him so much distress in his 'passion for gain' (85) that he finally implores his patron to restore him to his former life-style. Here, for a moment, we have a pleasant portrayal of life in the city—a blend of work and leisure (56–9)—and a picture of the hard work and set-backs involved in farming (83–7). But the central message is the same as ever—the aims of life are *otium* and independence. It is interesting to see that the city-country contrast can be used to make the same points in two very different and virtually antithetical versions. This supports the view that the portrayals of city and country life in Roman satire are not included for their simple descriptive or documentary value but serve a purpose, and in so doing reveal aspects of Roman ideology.

And in fact Horace goes on in *Epistles* 1.11 to suggest that location cannot provide you with peace of mind, because this comes from within. This point is picked up in yet another of Horace's poems in *Epistles* 1 which features a city/country antithesis: *Epistles* 1.14. Here Horace contrasts his own love of the country with his bailiff's longing for the city. He uses by now fairly familiar stereotypes—the wild and beautiful countryside (line 20), the idyllic countryside (line 35), the tasks of the countryside (lines 27–30 and 39), the seedy aspects of city life (lines 21–6), not so much to evoke the familiar moral contrast between city and country as to argue that envy of someone else's situation is foolish (lines 40–4) and that happiness is a state of mind (lines 11–13).[44]

Persius on city and country

In Persius we find very little that is conventional and clichéd. There is no sustained condemnation of city life as such, but the pictures of corruption and so on are generally set in the city. This is sometimes indicated by a single word which gives a fleeting glimpse of a city scenario, e.g. the Tiber (2.16), the Subura (5.33) and the Festival of Flora (5.179). Other scenes are ones for which we can assume a city setting, for example the poetry recitation (1.15–21), the court scene (1.83–91), the soldier's mockery of philosophers (3.77–87) and others. The nearest we get to the topos of the idyllic country existence is at the beginning of Satire 6, where Persius describes his winter retreat in Liguria: for him the place brings happiness and freedom from resentment. Again, the country is used in its role as morally superior to the city—here to present a speaker who subscribes to the 'enjoy what you have' (line 22) view of life and who detaches himself from the obligations of Roman life, in particular the obligation to one's heir not to diminish the inheritance by extravagant—or simply comfortable—living.[45] Only in one other passage does Persius provide more than a fleeting glimpse of the country, in Satire 1 where he criticises the inadequacy of contemporary poets. In lines 69–75 this criticism is couched in terms of their inability to describe country scenes—the grove, the farm, the country festival:

> Just look, we are teaching them to voice heroic sentiments—amateurs who used to doodle in Greek! They haven't the skill to depict a clump of trees or the

well-fed land with its baskets and hearths and pigs, and the hay smoking on Pales' holiday, from which came Remus and Cincinnatus, who was polishing his share in the furrow when his flustered wife, with a quorum of oxen, invested him Dictator, and the sergeant took home the plough.

These country scenes he declares to have been the origin of early military leaders of Rome such as Cincinnatus. This detail is not superfluous: it establishes the moral superiority of the country, by linking or identifying the moral excellence of the past with the moral excellence of the countryside. Persius seems to be using the country to symbolise what is real and substantial and valuable as the antithesis of the concerns of contemporary poetry, which he condemns as artificial and trivial and worthless.

More moral symbolism in Juvenal

Returning to Juvenal, we find a similar use of city and country as vehicles of moral comment. In the opening to Satire 6 and again in lines 286ff., Juvenal uses the country as a symbol of moral purity in contrast with the corruption and decadence of the city. At the start of the poem, Juvenal suggests that Chastity existed during the Golden Age, when people inhabited cave-dwellings along with their animals, by contrast with modern-day Rome, which is characterised by neurotic, sophisticated and promiscuous women, such as those described by the love-elegists. The fact that the picture of the Golden Age woman is rather ambivalent—'shaggier than her acorn-belching husband'—does not detract from the prime function of this Golden Age country scene; it simply adds a satirist's typical deflation. The same contrast occurs, but a little updated, at 286ff. Here the life of Latin women in the time of the Second Punic War (218–201 B.C.) is characterised by chastity and poverty and hard work and contrasted with modern-day Rome which is tainted by Luxury and the crime and lust it brings. None of this is evidence for conditions of life in Latium in the time of Hannibal or in Rome under the Empire: it is part of the conventional analysis of decline. A classic example of such analysis occurs in Sallust, *Catiline* 10:[46]

> But when the state had grown through hard work and exercising justice, when great kings had been overcome in war, savage tribes and mighty peoples had been subdued by force, when Carthage, the rival of Roman power, had been annihilated and all seas and lands lay open, then Fortune began cruelly to throw everything into turmoil. People who had found it easy to endure hard work, dangers, anxiety and set-backs found leisure and riches (desirable in other circumstances) a burden and a curse. So the desire first for money then for power

grew; this was, so to speak, the root of all evils. For greed destroyed trust, integrity and other noble qualities, and in their place taught men to be arrogant, cruel, to neglect the gods and to set a price on everything. Ambition drove many men to become false, to have one thing hidden in their hearts and another ready on the tongue, to value friendships and enmities not on their merits but according to advantage, and to show a good face rather than a good character. At first these vices grew little by little; from time to time they were punished; finally, when the disease had spread like the plague, the state was changed and government turned from being the best and most just into one cruel and unendurable.

Satire 11 shows a similar exploitation of the country with its evocation of the simple and natural and native. In this poem, which is in effect an invitation to a friend to dinner, Juvenal cleverly creates a *country* meal—such as that envisaged by Horace in Satire 2.6—in a *city* setting. He promises that the meal will consist of 'courses supplied by no markets' from his 'farm at Tivoli' (lines 64–5). The ideological value, the moral superiority with which this food is invested, makes it very difficult to use this as 'hard' evidence. Only where details are corroborated in an author with no ideological point to make can one believe them. Moreover, we should not use this poem to prove that Juvenal had an estate at Tivoli.[47] This is cited as a typical place in the countryside, not too remote from Rome (20 miles), where a well-off Roman might have a villa.[48] And when we notice that literary men traditionally had farms in the Campagna, for example, Horace, Martial, Statius, it becomes very unclear whether we have here a traditional literary fiction or socio-economic reality—or both.[49]

After describing evocatively some of the attractive country fare they will enjoy at their meal, Juvenal proceeds to a picture of the good old days, when a feast such as he has just described would have been regarded as more than fit for a king. As in Satire 6 and Persius 1, we see that idealisation of rustic values often coincides in Roman thought with idealisation of the past. The contrast is expressed succinctly:

> Curius[50] used to put on his modest hearth with his own hands the simple vegetables he had gathered in his little garden, vegetables such as nowadays the dirty chain-gang ditcher in his great shackles who calls to mind the flavour of tripe in the warm café turns up his nose at. (Juv. 11.78-81)[51]

The description which follows of a festival day feast in the good old days recalls the efforts which the country mouse goes to in Horace 2.6 to make his meal special: on both occasions bacon fat (*lardum*) is specified as the crowning glory of the meal (Juv. 11.84 and Hor. *Sat.* 2.6.85). The following picture of the former consul and dictator returning home from working the fields with his spade on his shoulder (86–9) is a standard picture which again uses good honest toil to link the symbolic value of country life with Rome's past greatness.[52]

And so on. The same values emerge yet again from the description of the slaves. Like the food, they are native and not foreign, homegrown and not bought, from the country and not the city and therefore not spoiled by city trends and manners:

> there will be no Phrygian or Lycian slave, none bought from a dealer at a great price; when you ask for anything, ask in Latin ... One is the son of a hardy shepherd, another of a cattle-man; he sighs for his mother, whom he has not seen for a long time, and wistfully longs for the little cottage and the well-known kids ... (11.147–53)

The wine has an identical pedigree to the food and slave who 'will hand you wines bottled on the very hills from which he himself comes, beneath whose top he played' (11.159–60). In short, 'Juvenal' is inviting his friend to a country banquet which is, paradoxically, set in the city. The meal is marked by the simplicity of the food and household and the absence of the fashions and strict rules of conduct characteristic of the city. The horrors of city life are for the most part left implicit; the points he dwells on—the obsession with luxurious dining-tables (120–9), the fashion for elaborate carving (136–41) and the salacious entertainment provided by Spanish dancing girls (162–70)—can hardly be called 'horrors' but, rather, criticise the slavish following of fashion. The only possible horror is the crowded and noisy Circus: 'all of Rome today is in the Circus, and a roar strikes my ear from which I gather that the Green has won' (11.197–8), which epitomises the crowdedness, the noise, the competitiveness and, again, the fashion-following typical of city life. 'Juvenal' deliberately avoids this and by contrast emphasises the importance of pleasing oneself and enjoying life and adopts, appropriately enough, a more Horatian tone of voice to evoke the qualities which Horace locates in the country. The poem presents an interesting twist to an old theme—and to give the praises of country life a city setting shows very clearly how unreliable such pictures are as evidence of 'everyday life'.[53]

Satirists and the Law

J. Duncan Cloud

The law does not play a major part in the world which the three surviving
Roman satirists have constructed for their readers, though, as we shall see,
its role in Horace is more significant, but it does provide us with a
touchstone for analysing their satirical strategies; for, by contrast with many
other aspects of Roman life, we can test the data in the satirists against an
alternative source of information, the professional and other legal literature
of which a considerable amount still survives.

The professional literature consists of three types. The first, and for our
purposes, the most important, are the books deriving from the legislative
activities of the emperor Justinian I (A.D. 527–565). At the end of A.D.
530 he set up a commission to produce an edition of useful excerpts from
the great classical jurists of the second and third centuries A.D. These were
published at the end of A.D. 533 as the *Digest*, a systematic arrangement
of legal texts which henceforth, along with an elementary text-book, the
Institutes, and a collection of imperial decisions, the *Code*, was to govern
the day-to-day law of the late Empire. The *Digest* is large (50 books) and
comprehensive; moreover, we are fortunate in possessing a manuscript of it,
admittedly rather carelessly copied, which probably dates from Justinian's
lifetime. The chief disadvantage of this extremely valuable source is that
it contains three strata spanning some seven centuries. The top stratum is
the sixth century A.D. The lawyers employed by Justinian were encouraged
by the emperor (*Deo Auctore*, 7) to update their sources where necessary
to reflect the contemporary legal situation and they did so, though on a
more modest scale than used to be supposed. Secondly, there is a stratum
covering mainly the second and third centuries A.D., when the legal
authorities excerpted for the *Digest* wrote their books. The bottom stratum
stretches from the third century B.C. to the second century A.D. and
consists of statutes, decrees of the senate and other forms of law which
entered the Roman legal system during this period and provided the texts
on which the great lawyers were commenting in their books. Thus there
are two stages at which deformation of the original material could and did

take place—between the second / third centuries and A.D. 533 and between the original appearance of the statute or other source of law and the date of the jurist's book from which the excerpt was taken.[1] The great jurists themselves were, reasonably enough, mainly interested in the law, largely the civil law, as it existed in their own day; this overlapped with Juvenal's lifetime, but not that of Horace in whose *Satires* and *Epistles* civil law is more important than it is in Persius or Juvenal.

It may be thought, after this preamble, that the *Digest* will prove almost wholly useless as a tool for examining the works of Horace and Juvenal, but this is not so, partly because the interpolated material is generally obvious but also because of a quite substantial quantity of other legal work dating from before the sixth century. The most valuable single item is a second-century A.D. elementary text-book, the *Institutes* of Gaius. This can be used to check whether the doctrine in the law books inspired by Justinian really goes back to the second and third centuries A.D., the classical period of Roman law, as it purports to do. There are also a number of other small works which sometimes contain the same excerpts as the *Digest* and thus act as a check on the accuracy of its citations.

There is a third class of legal source—the law at work, for example in the speeches of Cicero, or preserved on Egyptian papyri or on wooden tablets recovered from Pompeii and Herculaneum where they had been buried as a result of the eruption of Mount Vesuvius in A.D. 79. This too has a direct bearing on our investigations, but it also enables us to correct and fill out the information in our first and second class of source. So, in sum, we have a large amount of material against which to check the accuracy of our three satirists; if we can find in any of them information which is factually false, we ought to be very chary of using that satirist as a source for Roman legal history.

Persius: inheritance, lawyers' fees, manumission

For the purposes of this book, Persius, though still significant, is the least important, because in his satires legal references are rare, as indeed one would expect. Persius' speaker, unlike the indignant moralist of Juvenal's first two books, is not interested in crime but in ethical questions, nor does Persius follow Horace's example in occasionally using legal imagery as a form of structural glue. Nevertheless, perhaps precisely because he is not much interested in the law, his use of legal material, which sometimes looks backwards to Horace's technique, sometimes forwards to Juvenal's, will help us to classify the procedures used by the satirists in their work and have some value laterally for their distortion of reality in other spheres.

In Persius' second Satire the speaker is concerned with the wrong and the right objects of prayer and gives some examples of discreditable prayers:

> If only by favour of Hercules I could find my harrow clonking against a preserving jar full of silver! Or how I wish I could obliterate my ward; I am hard on his heels as heir nearest in succession and he is mangy and swollen with bile. Nerius is already burying his third wife. (2.10–14)

The situation appears legally quite straightforward; the tutor is successor to his ward; in his prayers he suggests to the gods that to terminate the ward's life would be an act of kindness to so sickly a youth. If 'Nerius is already . . .' is part of the same prayer and not a separate one that his wealthy wife may die, then it offers the gods a precedent for intervention; Nerius has acquired the personal dowries of two wives and is on the point of acquiring that of his third—between the tutor and wealth stands only one sickly youth. The only significant item legally is Persius' choice of the phrase 'heir nearest in succession', *proximus heres*, which is a mixture of two legal phrases, *agnatus proximus*, the closest relative in the male line whose claim on the estate of a man who had died without making a will was likely to come next after the child or children, and *secundus heres*, heir in default named in a person's will. The two phrases thus assume different contexts—the first the situation after the death of a man who has not made a will, the second that arising after the death of someone who *has* made a will. The conflation of the two phrases could merely be a signal from the satirist that he is writing satire, not a commentary on the law of testate and/or intestate succession. But the conflation is elegant as well. The use of *secundus* would have given us an exact echo of Horace's phrase in *Sat.* 2.5.44–50 where a legacy-hunter gets himself made heir in default (*heres secundus*) when the first heir is a sickly child. There would then have been Persius' usual play with a Horatian subtext, for Horace's legacy-hunter is heir in default to a genuinely sickly boy and thus has no need to pray; there is a fair likelihood that in the order of nature some mischance will eventually thrust him down to Hades (49). Persius' tutor's ward merely has eczema and dyspepsia; thus the tutor's prayer is more disreputable than the opportunism of Horace's legacy-hunter—the tutor's is a quasi-parental relationship and his potential victim is well enough for the tutor to require some help from Olympus in order to ensure the ward's premature demise. The substitution of *proximus* retains the play with the Horatian passage but adds a touch which is both heightening and distancing—heightening because the tutor is actually the ward's closest blood-relation and at the same time distancing, because Persius' phrase, unlike Horace's, evokes the legal world of the Twelve Tables, half a millennium earlier, which established the rule that the closest relation in the male line, the *agnatus proximus*, automatically became the future heir's tutor in cases of intestacy and in the event of his death inherited.[2] By evoking the world of the fifth century B.C. rather than contemporary law Persius can contrast ironically—'to make sure these prayers are holy' (15)—the hallowed context of shrine and guardianship with the sinister shabbiness of the prayer; he can also play games with Horatian subtexts.[3] Lastly, he can manipulate his favourite images of disease[4], again ironically, for it is the guardian who is mangy quite as much as the ward. In short, Persius conflates two standard legal phrases in order to combine the maximum number of historical and literary resonances; accuracy is sacrificed to poetry.

My next example (3.73–6) describes the payment of a barrister in kind; jars of food, the pay-off for his defence of some fat Umbrians, rot in his larder, while a Marsian client gives him pepper, hams and sprats by the barrelful. The sprat is an unlikely gift from a client in the Apennines; it owes its presence to Lucilius (1033W), just as the pepper and the rotting jar derive from Horace (*Sat.* 2.4.66 and 74). What appears to be a precise account of payment in kind dissolves into graceful allusion to Persius' two satiric predecessors, leaving us with a lingering doubt not just about the details but about the institution itself. The payment of a maximum fee to barristers of 10,000 sesterces had been fixed by the emperor Claudius in A.D. 47 and one would have expected the fat Umbrians to pay cash.[5] It is possible that Persius is referring to presents over and above the lawyer's fee, but he does not say so and I suspect this passage is a reworking of a theme which goes back to Lucilius; in the latter's day the payment of fees to barristers was forbidden by the *lex Cincia* of 204 B.C.; payment in kind was a way of getting round the law in Cicero's day by those who still had scruples over contravening the Cincian Law[6] and it must have been the same three-quarters of a century earlier than Cicero, when Lucilius was writing his satires.

Persius' only sustained engagement with the law comes in the latter part of Satire 5 (73 ff.) where there is a sustained contrast between real and legal freedom. One common method by which a slave obtained his freedom in the early Empire was manumission by will to which Persius refers elsewhere (3.105–6). Here Persius uses as his model another form of manumission, manumission 'by the rod' (*uindicta*). The speaker's argument is that the magistrate, the urban praetor, cannot confer real freedom, even in the terms used by the law-books (*cp. Dig.* 1.5.4.*pr.*: 'Freedom is the natural faculty of doing anything one pleases except what is prevented by force or law'), since a fool cannot make a rational choice: Dama remains Dama even when he has become Marcus Dama, gaining the *praenomen* Marcus as a sign of his citizenship.

It is worth considering why Persius chooses manumission by the rod to make his point. A somewhat superficial reason is that the form of manumission which involves the principal magistrate concerned with law, the urban praetor, makes a more elegant prelude to the list of functions that Dama, now a Roman citizen, will be able to perform (79–81), namely acting as security for a loan, sitting on the bench and witnessing wills. But there is a second reason: this form of manumission is based on two legal fictions, (1) that the slave was reclaiming freedom of which he had been wrongfully deprived, and (2) that the citizen claiming on his behalf was recovering his property from the slave's owner. But for the speaker manumission is a moral sham: a slave who has been given his freedom does not suddenly become a reliable guarantor of a loan or an honest *iudex*.[7] Consequently the model of manumission which is based on a pair of fictions makes a satisfying symbol for an institution which, the speaker argues, is itself a sham. A further feature drives home the point: the owner turns the slave round (76, 78). This is the only symbolic act, apart from the use of the rod (*uindicta*) which gives its name to the form of manumission, to which the satirist refers and he mentions it three times! And yet it is not alluded to in the legal sources at all. However, since it is mentioned by Seneca (*Ep.* 8.7) and Appian (*BC* 4.135) as well as by Persius, it clearly occurred, though presumably as an optional extra. Persius, in describing the action in terms of the word 'dizzy-turn' and '(gyrating) top',[8] emphasises hyperbolically its dizzying speed. The action, which was probably intended to symbolise the slave's metamorphosis into free man,[9] becomes the senseless whizzing of a top; the change of status induces dizziness, not wisdom or virtue.

Juvenal's (mis-)use of the law

Persius' infrequent incursions into the realm of law and lawyers involve everything from what looks suspiciously like fiction to the recording of detail not given in our legal sources, but in each case the deployment of the material is dictated not by the desire to provide us with insights into the working of the Roman legal system under the emperor Nero but by the needs of the poem and the rules of the literary form, in this case satire. There is another point which cannot be repeated too often—Roman

satirists, like their modern successors, are out to entertain. Persius (*Sat.*
1.116–23) and Horace (*Sat.* 1.1.23–6, 10.7–8, 11, 14–15) say so and though
Juvenal does not lay claim to a sense of the ridiculous as his satirical
approach before Satire 10 (31–53), his earlier satires are as obviously meant
to be entertaining as were those of his predecessors. It is funnier to think
of the speaker in Persius' third Satire being paid in sprats rather than
sesterces, just as it is more entertaining to think of Dama being twirled
into the citizenship instead of being left his freedom in his owner's will.
The joke's the thing, not actuality. Barristers were not paid in sprats in
Persius' day, whereas slaves *were* freed by the rod. The choice between
actuality and anachronism is dictated by humour and by point. Juvenal's
approach to the law is even more flexible; having signalled at the beginning
of his first, programmatic, satire that he will adapt the techniques of the
declamatory schools to the needs of satire, he leads us to expect a similar
use of legal material: in the declamations preserved by the elder Seneca or
attributed to Quintilian 'the law' is a blend of Roman and Greek law mixed
in with pure fantasy. In the case of Juvenal there are no Greek elements,
nor would one expect them, since all the 'masks' adopted by the satirist
involve in differing degrees a hostility towards the Greeks. But in other
respects he adopts the declaimers' playful attitude to legal reality.

Juvenal uses legal material in three, not always distinct, ways: to heighten
the emotional tone, to provide an element in a vignette and (in two longer
passages) to exemplify or furnish a satirical theme.

Since the speaker in Juvenal's *Satires*, and particularly the unbalanced
moralist who lectures us in *Satires* 1–6, is concerned with human depravity,
the law offers one standard against which human beings offend. It is natural
in view of the grander tone of Juvenal's *Satires* that a good deal of his
material is drawn from the statutes of Roman public law, whereas Horace
and Persius draw, perhaps exclusively, on civil law material. And given the
preoccupation with materialism, sex and violence that characterises the
indignant moralist and, to a lesser degree, the more detached speakers of
the later satires, it is not surprising that the legal input into the tirades is
provided by inheritance legislation (1.55–6) and the Roscian law on the
theatre which gave non-senators with a capital of at least 400,000 sesterces
the right to sit in the first fourteen tiers at the theatre (3.155; 14.324), the
Augustan law on adultery and the Scantinian law which concern themselves
with deviation from accepted norms of sexual behaviour (2.29, 37, 44;
10.315) and assault and battery (*iniuria*) (3.288; 16.7–34). There is a slight
danger even here for the social historian who is unaware of Juvenal's
techniques. There is good evidence to suppose that Domitian enforced not

only a law like the adultery statute (*lex Iulia de adulteriis*) which was still on the statute book but even revived the obsolete Scantinian law against sodomy.[10] This last is never heard of again and there is no reason to suppose that its employment survived Domitian's assassination, any more than the food-dole (*sportula*) which, in the same spirit of archaism, he revived in place of cash handouts. Now Juvenal has a habit of placing some of his satires in a vaguely past time in a way similar to the use of a vaguely late Victorian context by Ivy Compton-Burnett in her novels, and of none is this more true than the second satire where the Domitianic environment is conveyed not only by direct reference to Domitian's recent (*nuper*) incest with his niece, but by allusions to his Dacian campaigns and to Agricola's recently (*modo*) conducted military operations in Scotland (2.1–2, 29–32, 37, 44, 159–61). It would therefore be very rash to infer from the probable publication date of Book I (= Satires 1–5) in the second decade of the second century that the Scantinian law continued in use. There was no need for it, since the *lex Iulia de adulteriis* punished all forms of illicit sex (*stuprum*), not simply adultery; only in the Domitianic era would there be historical sense in Laronia's riposte to the hypocritical homosexual moralist who had been calling for a stiffer use of the *lex Iulia* against loose women, that, since male homosexuals are more outrageous offenders, the Scantinian law should be invoked first. The reference to the Scantinian law is a joke.

Failure to take into consideration Juvenal's elastic use of time has caused trouble elsewhere. In 1.55–7 there is a vignette of a husband pretending to be asleep over his cups while his wife is carrying on with her lover, since she has no legal right to inherit (*si capiendi | ius nullum uxori*). Presumably we must look for a situation in which a husband in return for a share in the inheritance to be left by his wife's lover agrees to pass on the rest to his wife; the arrangement is necessary because she is for some reason barred from inheriting herself. Several points are worth making here. First, the notion that arouses the rage of the speaker is that of a husband acting as pimp (*leno*) for his wife; the speaker imagines that the reason for the husband's behaviour is that his wife lacks the right of inheritance, but the reason for the speaker's rage, as so often, is that materialistic values have inverted traditional values—for the sake of financial gain a husband turns himself into a pimp and a voyeur. The legal niceties are of no importance. Secondly, a very similar situation provided the theme for a declamation ([Quintil.] *Decl.* 325): the lover institutes the husband as heir and after the lover's death the wife takes the husband to court on the ground that the inheritance was really a trust (*fideicommissum*) intended for her. So we are dealing with a variation on a declamatory theme, as well as a variation on a Lucilian theme (251W), rather than a real life situation. In real life, a lover wishing to leave his estate to his mistress who lacks the right of inheritance would not have got round the law by making her husband the trustee of a trust of which she was sole beneficiary; he would have chosen someone else, in view of Roman Law's suspicion of financial arrangements entered into between spouses. In any case, by Juvenal's day trusts set up to circumvent the inheritance laws were, to all intents and purposes, illegal. So presumably the speaker in the satire is referring to a secret trust (tacit *fideicommissum*) whereby the husband made a verbal promise to hand over the inheritance to his wife. But such arrangements were fraudulent, if their purpose was to enable someone to *de facto* inherit when debarred by law from inheriting (*Dig.* 34.9.10 *pr.*) which is precisely the lover's intention in Juvenal. So in real life, as indeed in the declamation, the lover could never have been certain that the husband would pass on the estate to his wife after the lover's death. At best, the wife as beneficiary would have been permitted to delate herself to the treasury and in return for her honesty or prudence would have been allowed to keep half or more exactly three eighths of the estate, the rest being confiscated to the treasury. But once we have reached this point, it becomes obvious that Juvenal is not really concerned at all with the law governing trusts, formal or informal. Consequently, it does seem rather a waste of time to speculate on the circumstances in which a husband could inherit, but not his wife. However, this rather obvious point has not stopped commentators on Juvenal and indeed the occasional contemporary writer on Roman Law like Marongiu[11] from indulging in precisely that sort of speculation. Three suggestions have been made: (1) the lover belongs to the highest class of citizens (the *classici*) and is forbidden by the Voconian Law of 169 B.C. to make any woman his heir; (2) under the *lex Papia Poppaea* of A.D. 9 wives had to have three children to inherit, husbands only one; this couple had one or two children; (3) the wife was a disreputable woman (*femina probrosa*) and debarred as such by Domitian from accepting legacies or inheritances. But (1) won't do: the *lex Voconia* was obsolete by the era of Juvenal.[12] Nor will (2) stand up; Gaius *Inst.* 2. 111 and 286a and *Dig.* 50.16.148 are unequivocal —it is childless married persons (*orbi*) who can only take half of any gifts, and the possession of even one child takes away the status of childlessness; thus, either *both* husband and wife will be penalised or neither of them.[13] As for (3), it proves either too little or too much; if Domitian did remove from disreputable women the right to inherit or receive legacies, as Suetonius (*Dom.* 8.3) states, then he must also have insisted on the removal of their right to benefit from *fideicommissa*; otherwise, his rescript would have been a dead letter *ab initio*. In short, none of these solutions works; the closest one can get to a genuine legal context is some point in the second century B.C. after the passing of the *lex Voconia* but before the possibilities of the fideicommisary dodge had been devised. But then, the search for a genuine second century A.D. legal background is to miss the point of the passage.

I could with equal or more justice have included the previous citation as an example of Juvenal's use of the law in vignettes. It is a cautionary example: we need *always* to consider the satirical point of a passage. As we have seen, the point here is the husband behaving as procurer for his wife—it is one that has its roots not only in the declamatory literature but in Juvenal's satirical predecessors, as well as amatory poetry and anec-dotage.[14]

A similar case is to be found at 10.235–9. The speaker is descanting upon the miseries of old age. The old man cannot even recognise his own children; he disinherits his own flesh and blood and bequeaths his whole property to a veteran prostitute who has provided him with oral sex. The reader is not meant to take this seriously—the speaker has already said (204–8) that old men are incapable of any kind of sex. In any case, Phiale, as a person of disreputable character (*persona turpis*) would have insuperable problems in defending herself in court against a complaint by the dis-inherited children that the will was undutiful *(querela inofficiosi testamenti)*; indeed, the children would have been entitled to a quarter even if Phiale had been perfectly respectable. But the speaker can make a more rhet-orically effective point about the disabilities of old age, if the old man not merely disinherits his children but disinherits them in favour of a prostitute and one who is no *poule de luxe* but old (she has been in business *multis annis*), occupying smelly underground premises and expert in unnatural practices!

On the other hand, where there is a dispute about some aspect of Roman legal history, we may very hesitantly use Juvenal to support one side or the other, if the point of the passage is improved by one interpretation rather than the other. A possible example of general interest is provided by Juvenal's two references to intestacy. It used to be the received opinion that the Romans had a horror of intestacy or dying without having made a will, but this view has become the subject of vigorous debate since the war.[15] It seems to me that the traditional view is the more likely to be right,[16] but my purpose here is to see whether Juvenal's indignant moralist can shed any light on the question.

The Latin word *intestatus* (normally meaning 'intestate') occurs twice in Juvenal. The first instance is problematic. In the first satire the moralist, who has attacked the rich man for eating large and expensive meals without sharing them with his dependants, states that as a result come sudden deaths and an old age which is *intestata*. 'A new and rather amusing story goes the rounds of all the supper-parties; the funeral is carried out to the applause of his angry friends.' (142–6) Interpreters have made very heavy weather of this passage; Housman thought that *intestata* old age meant '*unattested* old age', i.e. that few rich men live to old age. But *intestatus* as an adjective meaning 'unattested' is exceedingly rare; the adjective normally means 'intestate' and that is what it has to mean on its only other appearance in Juvenal. At the very least, *intestata senectus* must *suggest* 'intestate old age'.[17] But in fact there is no reason to think that *intestata* here means anything other than '*intestate old age.*' The old man dies suddenly without having had time to make his will; he has put off making his will to the last minute, like Horace (cf. n.16), but in his case to keep his 'friends' (*amici*, here a euphemism for 'clients'), on tenterhooks. They are angry because he has not left them any legacies, but they are pleased that so mean an individual has got his come-uppance: a premature death with the stigma of intestacy thrown in.

In this case doubts about the meaning of *intestatus* make it unwise to push the argument very far, but at 3.272–5 there is no doubt about what *intestatus* means. Umbricius, warming to the horrors of life in Rome, declares that people are always throwing broken pots from the upper windows of their houses; falling from such a height they leave dents in the pavement. 'You could be regarded as unbusinesslike and careless of unforeseen accident (*ignauus . . . et subiti casus improuidus*) if you go out to dinner without making your will (*intestatus*). So true is it that there are as many sources of death as there are open windows with people awake behind them, as you pass by.' The implications are plain; a businesslike and provident person makes his will when in danger of death but this comment makes no sense if intestacy is regarded as normal and natural. What is more, Umbricius has in mind the poor, not the rich citizen, one who cannot afford a proper lantern (286–7) and is accused by a mugger of stuffing himself on beans, vinegar and a boiled sheep's head in a cobbler's company (292–4), thus suggesting that the poor as well as the rich were expected to make a will, contrary to Daube's general thesis that the Roman poor do not make wills.

Of course, what Juvenal's speakers say is not necessarily true; indeed, part of the fun is the mixture of fact and fantasy. Here the fantasy is that the insomniac tenement dwellers are only waiting for Umbricius to pass by in order to heave grandma's battered amphora on to his unsuspecting head. But if people did not normally make a will when in imminent danger of death, then the joke would be weakened, not strengthened. We may therefore cite Juvenal in support of the traditional view that Romans abhorred intestacy.

Juvenal's 'poor' barristers; Juvenal and military law

Finally, two longer passages deserve scrutiny. The first, in Satire 7, a satire dealing with the unprofitability of literature and the respectable professions, devotes some forty lines (106–49) to the miserable lot of barristers: only the barrister who is upper-class and rich can name his fee; consequently the barrister either goes bankrupt in the effort to keep up appearances or lives miserably on gifts in kind or on paltry fees, most of which go to his legal advisors (*pragmatici*). The speaker makes his points in Juvenal's usual entertaining way.[18] Some of the elements in the picture receive support from other sources: barristers were expected to put on a show (Pliny *Ep.* 6.32.1) and did go in for equestrian statues of themselves (Martial 9.68.6). However, on the main issue—the poverty of all but a few upper-class barristers (*patroni*)—the speaker is simply wrong. Martial can say: 'If you want to be rich, become a lawyer' (2.30.5) and the baker turned barrister who charged his client 200,000 sesterces (8.16) was no patrician Aemilius.[19] The barrister who was paid 10,000 sesterces to represent the municipality of Vicenza and then failed to turn up in court, Tuscilius Nominatus, was no Aemilius either (Pliny *Ep.*5.4 and 13); moreover, the debate in the Senate reported in the second letter suggests that chicanery and rapacity were rampant in the legal profession. So the other evidence strongly suggests that the speaker in Juvenal's seventh Satire is wrong in asserting that poverty was the lot of most lawyers, though, of course, it suits the speaker's purpose to make the assertion.

What is more, I think that we can document a phenomenon which appears elsewhere in Juvenal,[20] namely the placing together of two social facts in such a way as to make a compound which is pure fantasy; in this case, the two social facts are (1) the giving of presents of food and drink to barristers at the festival of the Saturnalia, a December festival at which, as at our Christmas, it was customary to give presents and (2) the payment of barristers for their services; the fantasy-compound is the payment of lawyers in kind. We have evidence for presents at the Saturnalia, mostly of food, to barristers in Martial 4.46. At Sat. 7.119–21 Juvenal lists the payment in kind to a barrister for bursting his guts in pleading a case before some clod of a *iudex*; the stale shallots and the flagons (*lagonae*) of wine from the upper Tiber valley derive from the Martial poem, though the choice of district for the very ordinary local *ordinaire* is a common-place of Satire and in Martial.[21] The jar of minute fish and the desiccated ham derive from the Persius passage cited earlier. That passage, it was argued, is either a reworking of a commonplace in Lucilius, when payment in kind did occur so as to avoid formal contravention of the *lex Cincia* forbidding the payment of fees to barristers, or just possibly a reference to presents, as in the Martial epigram. What it cannot be is a statement about contemporary methods used by the rich to pay their lawyers; as we have seen, payments in cash were now legitimate and there is good reason to suppose that the upper limit of 10,000 sesterces could be breached. Eprius Marcellus and Vibius Crispus hardly made fortunes of two hundred and three hundred million sesterces (Tacitus *Dialogus* 8) out of 10,000 sesterces fees, even if we take into consideration the proceeds from their careers as informers/prosecutors (*delatores*) in treason trials. We have already noted Martial's ex-baker charging a client 200,000 sesterces. Almost certainly, then, Juvenal is mingling Martial's statement about presents to advocates with a *topos* about payment in kind which no longer represented contemporary practice in Nero's principate and *a fortiori* in Hadrian's. Martial (3.38.5–6) attests payment of lawyers on the instalment plan (and the client's habit of defaulting on the instalments); such an instalment scheme would make it possible for even a very humble client to pay cash for a lawyer's services.

The second long passage occurs in Satire 16 and is concerned, this time, not with lawyers but with the law; indeed, it is unique in extant Roman satire in that fifty consecutive lines (7–56) are devoted to points of law, namely the legal advantages enjoyed by soldiers. Unfortunately, the poem breaks off in the middle of a sentence at line 60; when we compare the number of lines in Book 5 with those in the other Books it is clear that a good deal must be missing. Consequently, we do not know how the three advantages the speaker ascribes to the military fitted into the overall structure of the poem nor can we be certain of the tone of the poem from the fragment that remains. Three points are made: (1) in the case of a civilian summonsing a soldier for assault and battery, the judge who hears the case is a centurion and the case takes place at camp; consequently, both judge and environment favour the defendant; (2) when a soldier brings an action, it is heard promptly, whereas for the civilian there are interminable delays; (3) a soldier can make a will during the lifetime of his father and can dispose of the money earned by his soldiering, whereas the civilian son with a father still living (*filius familias*) cannot make a will. Only the third of these privileges is attested in the legal literature (Gaius *Inst.* 2. 106; *Dig.* 29.1.11). Juvenal has his facts right, but has fastened on a relatively unimportant feature; the most important privilege attaching to a military will was its freedom from the formal and other restrictions hemming about the civilian will. For example, a serving soldier with children could have left his money to the Phiale of Satire 10 and there would have been nothing the children could do about it. It is clearly the paradoxical character of the consequences of a military son being able to make a will that appeals to the speaker; nature and the traditional order of society are inverted when the elderly father hunts a legacy from his son (56), a theme which, with the younger man's name, Coranus, was taken over from Horace *Sat.* 2.5.55–69.

The first privilege is the most dubiously historical. There is no other evidence that in cases where soldiers litigated with civilians, the case had to be heard by a military judge and within an army camp. It is in fact most unlikely that such a formal rule ever existed. The argument from silence is quite strong. The *Digest* (esp. 5.1) provides a good deal of material on the qualifications required by a *iudex*, yet there is absolutely nothing about military courts trying civilians. Again, we have no evidence that the urban praetor ever actually named a serving soldier as judge; there is some suspicious fudging on the speaker's part; he does not actually *say* that the praetor assigned a military judge. What he says is that the civilian roughed up by a soldier would pretend it had not happened and would not dare to show the praetor his knocked-out teeth etc. (9–10). Then 'to someone wishing to punish these things an Illyrian boot'—Illyrian boots were worn by soldiers or possibly N.C.O.s (*cf.* Martial 4.5.4)—'is assigned as judge' (13). In any case it is unlikely that the praetor's writ ran in army camps. Would he even have possessed a list of suitable centurions in his register (*album*) of eligible *iudices*?[22] The language of lines 15–17, 'The old camp regulations and practice of Camillus are still retained, that soldiers should not litigate outside the palisade and away from the standards' and of lines 25–7, 'Anyhow, who would support you in court[23] and be such a pal (*Pylades*)[24] as to go beyond the massive rampart?', suggests a frontier camp, but this is simply one of Juvenal's jokes: the scene of the punch-up must be Rome or its immediate environs. Otherwise, the victim would be unable to display his knocked-out teeth to the praetor, even if he wanted to. The sort of punch-up between soldier and civilian that Juvenal's listeners and readers in Rome would be likely to encounter would be one involving a citizen and a member of the praetorian guard, whose camp was less than a mile from the old wall of the city, to which the phrase 'massive rampart' could well refer.[25]

I think we can now begin to see what Juvenal is up to. It is a fact that when one soldier was in dispute with another soldier the camp prefect would assign a soldier of some status as adjudicator between them.[26] It is also a fact that when one citizen wished to bring an action against another civilian citizen the urban praetor would assign an adjudicator. What happened when a soldier and a civilian were in dispute we do not know, but probably the scene of the action was all important; within the camp, the camp prefect had jurisdiction, outside it the jurisdiction was the urban praetor's. The speaker has deliberately muddled up the two situations, to suggest firstly that even in Rome a citizen in conflict with a soldier might expect the rough justice of a frontier camp and secondly that soldiers had the whip-hand even in the civilian heart of the Empire, Rome.[27]

The middle section (35–50) provides another example of the satirist's slyness. There could certainly be delays in the completion of legal actions, but these must have been exceptional, not integral to the workings of the law as they were in Victorian Chancery cases, if only because of the rule, cited by Gaius (*Inst.* 4.104–5), that actions 'died' if they were not completed within eighteen months. No doubt, as Kelly suggests,[28] there were exceptions to cover special cases, but the satirist is very characteristically converting the exceptional case into a rule in suggesting that delays invariably occur and that it takes a year even to get started (42). On the other hand, we do not know whether the soldier's case was automatically heard at a time of his own convenience (48–50). Since there is no such rule in the legal literature, I suspect the satirist of once again erecting some special exception into a general rule.

To sum up, Juvenal's use of law is more complex than that of Persius, but fundamentally the same rules apply: the material runs from accurate fact to declamatory fiction. Before using Juvenal, the legal historian must always ask himself/herself: is the truth of the information essential to the point that the speaker is trying to make and have we any corroborative evidence for the 'fact' described? If the answer to both these questions is 'no', then the historian should ignore Juvenal altogether. Indeed, our examination of Juvenal's technique has obvious implications for historians outside the field of law.

Law in Horace: illustration, symbol, theme

Let us turn finally to Horace, for though first chronologically, he uses law not only in the same ways as the two later satirists but in other ways which his successors did not see fit to develop. The satirist's fictional world is very much, in edited form, that of the elite for which he wrote and in which certain aspects of law played a considerable part. Consequently, a certain number of legal references are there simply to convey an atmosphere of Roman normality. The opening poem, where Horace links dissatisfaction with one's lot and greed, serves as a pointer to the significance of the law in the satirist's scheme of things. Within the first ten lines we find the lawyer envying the farmer when an anxious client knocks him up at dawn, while the farmer, torn from his farm to answer bail in Rome, exclaims that true happiness is only to be found at Rome (*Sat.* 1.1.9–12). We shall see that the legal expert (*iuris peritus* or *consultus*) and bail (*uadimonium*) play crucial roles in the two satires where a legal theme runs through all or most of a poem. For the moment, it is only worth observing that Horace has signalled that he will use the law as illustration, symbol or theme throughout the Satires and to a smaller extent in the Epistles.

Illustration, symbol, theme. I will take each in turn, though with as subtle an artist as Horace, any one of them has a habit of turning into another.

In Satire 1.3 Horace is discussing equity, a sense of proportion in discriminating between one fault and another (76–124). That a good many of his illustrations will come from law is indicated by his sandwiching this section of the poem between the names of two contemporary jurists, Labeo (82) and Alfenus (130), the latter already celebrated and the former destined to be even more distinguished.[29] In the middle of the passage there is an Epicurean excursus on the origin of law, and unity is given to the passage by not only making theft the centre-piece of the excursus—'(Human beings when they had learnt the use of speech) thereafter began to abstain from war, construct walled towns, and lay down laws that no-one should be a thief or a brigand nor yet an adulterer'[30]—but by also making the punishment of theft the main example and symbol of dealing with sins (*peccata*) or failings (*uitia*): the slave who licks up some half-eaten piece of fish and some sauce (81), the man who steals a chicken from my dish (91–2), simple theft (94), stealing a cabbage from a kitchen-garden (116), removing sacred emblems (117, which is what, etymologically, sacrilege means) and brigandage contrasted with common theft (122). Theft and the law provides not only illustrative material; our common-sense response to theft refutes the Stoic dogma that all sins are equal. The man who hangs his slave for stealing a piece of half-eaten fish is crazy; it is irrational to regard the theft of a neighbour's young cabbage and the theft of sacred emblems, or ordinary theft and armed robbery, as sins equally grave. But the law itself distinguished between the gravity of different types of theft and thus law is symbol of the common-sense response as well as example of it.

This passage is fairly typical of one way in which Horace uses legal material; its function is partly ethical and partly structural. The satirist purports to be a teacher of morality and the law serves the same function. But, by the same token, the law can serve a structural purpose and hold together a whole passage by means of thematic reference. But however valuable such points may be to the literary analysis of Horace's technique, they are of little use to the historian of law. They shed no light on the way the law worked in the 30s B.C.; at most, we might want to argue that there was contemporary interest not only in the origins of law but in determining whether or not in the field of crime one could or should construct a scale of heinousness. Certainly, the question was one on which Epicureans and Stoics differed vigorously and Horace is pushing the Epicurean line. But as we can never be quite sure whether to take satirical preaching at its face value, we can equally never be quite sure whether its content reflects the cut and thrust of contemporary ethical dialectic or is meant to be absurd. A less elevated passage in the excursus on the origin of law arouses some doubts about the high moral seriousness of the preacher.[31]

In one sense, the range of legal reference in Horace is most impressive. A list, not necessarily complete, of areas covered by Horace in the Satires and Epistles would have to include testamentary law (*Sat.* 2.3.84–91 and 2.5 *passim*), credit and loans (*Sat.* 1.2.12–19, 1.3.86–9, 2.3.69–71 and 2.7.17–19; *Epist.* 1.7.80 (the form known as *mutui datio*) and 2.1.105), forms of surety (*sponsio*) and bail (*uadimonium*) (*Sat.*1.1.11, 1.3.95, 1.9.35–42, 2.6.23 and *Epist.* 1.16.43), fraud (*Epist.* 2.1.122), slavery (*Epist.*1.16.46–9, the sale of a slave, and 2.2.1–19), guardianship (*Sat.* 2.3.218; *Epist.* 1.1.102 (custody of a lunatic, *cura furiosi*), conveyancing (*Epist.* 2.2.158, the form known as *libra et aere* and 159–79 for other forms), libel (*Sat.* 2.1 *passim* and *Epist.* 2.1.152–3) and procedure in a civil action (*Sat.* 1.9.35–42, 74–8 and 2.5.27–35). Yet Horace's use of Roman Law is of little value to historians of Roman Law. To take some random samples which illustrate the way in which Horace makes use of his legal material, in *Epist.* 1.16.40–4 the good man is defined in terms of the legal obligations of a Roman citizen and the slave defines himself in terms of the offences he has not committed (46–9). In *Epist.* 2.2.2–24 Horace excuses his poor record as correspondent in a long simile based on the Roman law of sale: the purchaser of a slave has no remedy if the seller admitted defects before sale. Horace has been perfectly open to Florus about his indolence as a correspondent and thus the latter has no grounds for complaint when his letters are not answered. We have seen already that in Satire 2.5 Horace makes considerable use of testamentary law: this is inevitable because the satire recounts Tiresias' advice to Ulysses/Odysseus, when the latter is visiting the Underworld (see *Odyssey* 11), to recoup his fortunes by a career as a legacy-hunter. The role of the surety (*sponsor*) recurs (*Satire* 1.3.95; 2.6.23; *Epist.* 1.16.43; 2.2.67) because it was so frequent an activity for Roman citizens. Nevertheless, although the operations of law are frequently referred to in the Satires and Epistles of Horace, we learn nothing new about Roman Law from reading Horace. What we do learn is that reference to Roman Law enhances the Romanness of the Satires; we can see this more obviously than usual in Satire 2.5, which purports to be an encounter between Greeks in mythological time, but deals with a very Roman phenomenon, legacy-hunting (*captatio*) in terms so Roman that the centrepiece is an anecdote in which Coranus outwits the legacy-hunting Nasica (55–69), both parties unashamedly Roman, as is the language of the will which will finally crown Ulysses' success as a legacy-hunter and make him rich.[32]

Horace is much more concerned with the poetic effect that legal reference can achieve than in fidelity to legal fact. Sometimes, this shows simply in terms of incomprehensibility. In *Satire* 2.3.69–71 it is clear that Horace is describing the folly of lending money to a man with a mania for buying works of art, but, apart from the fact that no amount of legal precautions will prevent the lender from losing his money, nothing is clear, perhaps because the somewhat hysterical speaker is not clear himself. However, a more significant example of poetic licence occurs in Satire 1.9.

The problem of the pest

In Satire 1.9 the law plays an important role at both the narrative and the emblematic level. The pest who dogs the unwilling Horace's footsteps in the hopes of securing an introduction to Horace's influential patron, Maecenas, is also on bail to turn up in court that day. To Horace's obvious disappointment (35–42) the pest decides that acquiring Maecenas' patronage is more important than winning his case; however, Horace is eventually rescued by the plaintiff in the case who, after having gained Horace's agreement to act as a witness of arrest, hurries the pest away to court (74–8). Thanks to tablets discovered some years ago when the Pompeian section of the Autostrada was being built, we now know more about the Roman system of bail[33] and therefore about the legal background to the satire. Much was clear before: a Roman lawsuit was in two stages; the parties first met before the praetor who would clarify the legal form of the dispute between them and then remand the case to be decided by an adjudicator (*iudex*). It is certain that the episode at the end of the poem must refer to the appearance of the parties before the praetor.[34] It used to be thought that lines 35–41 referred to the second stage—the pest will lose his case before the *iudex* if he does not turn up. This interpretation led to critics having to resort to one of two unlikely explanations: the pest has two lawsuits on hand, but each is at different stages, or else Horace is being careless and 74–8 really refers to the second stage. Now there certainly are legal problems arising from the poem, but they are different from those in the traditional formulation. We now know that the two parties to an action would agree to appear at a certain place—here the Temple of Vesta—and proceed from there to the praetor's tribunal. The pest has promised the plaintiff that he will present himself at the agreed time and place: if he fails to do so, he will have to hand over a fixed sum of money to the plaintiff. Hence his perplexity; but he decides in the end that Maecenas' patronage will be more fruitful than winning his lawsuit. The only point that does not quite fit this interpretation is that Horace says (37) that if the pest fails to answer bail, he will lose his case (*litem*) whereas, strictly speaking, he will lose his bail-money rather than his case, for there will not be a case to lose.[35] However, the final episode in the little drama is still a puzzle; why should the plaintiff be so anxious to drag the pest off to court, if he could get his money automatically from the pest? Possibly double jeopardy? The plaintiff goes both for the bail money which was related to the sum at issue and for winning his case. But surely the pest could argue that as he had in fact turned up in court, he ought not to lose his bail. I think that the answer to the problem lies not in Roman law but the poetic intention of the satirist. Law plays an emblematic as well as a narrative role in the satire. 'Horace' is the representative of an orderly approach to conduct; the good man, as in *Epist.* 1.16.40 ff., is defined in terms of the right performance of his legal duties. The pest on the other hand outrages right order in every way; he is therefore shown first of all as one who ignores his legal obligation to answer bail and then, as is proper, the Law takes its revenge and rescues Horace. The emblematic role of law in this poem is as custodian of right order, right order in poetry as in personal behaviour. The pest is disorderly and order must be reestablished. The poem *needs* the violent reassertion of law that only the archaic ritual seizure of the defendant would provide, even if a real life Roman plaintiff would have been satisfied with the bail money and have left matters there.

There is some reason to think that the kind of violent seizure of defendant by plaintiff who then dragged him to court, as happens at the end of Satire 9, was unusual in the first century B.C. Bail was more civilised; all that remained of the ritual was the walking together of plaintiff and defendant from the agreed meeting-place to the praetor's tribunal.

A phoney legal consultation

A reference back to the legal position in much earlier times recurs in the last satire we shall consider. In the programmatic poem which commences the Second Book of Horace's Satires the satirist casts his attitude to satire in the form of a consultation with a celebrated lawyer of the day, C. Trebatius Testa. He is talking about the laws of satire (2)—and what could be more natural, in a jokey way, than to consult a lawyer about laws, even the laws of satire? What is more, the satirist purports to be concerned with the limits of personal criticism in satire, and, once again, who better to consult than a lawyer if one is worried about the law of libel? But although the satire takes the standard form of a legal consultation,[36] it is a parody and a funny parody at that; Roman clients did not consult their legal advisors about cures for insomnia nor is swimming across the Tiber three times much of a cure for insomnia, since it would have parted Horace from both his clothes and his bed! (lines 7–8). But the only law that Trebatius appeals to is the Twelve Tables which he quotes at line 82. That the Twelve Tables probably intended the clause to refer to putting spells on people, not writing libels, adds to the joke.[37] But the reference to the Twelve Tables is above all a signal to the reader/listener that the poem is not to be taken seriously *as a piece of law*. This has not stopped scholars from supposing that it provides evidence that Sulla's statute on assault and battery included defamation among the offences it punished![38]

In our end is our beginning. We found Persius using echoes of the Twelve Tables for his own poetic purposes and in this, as in so many other respects, he followed Horace.[39] The moral is clear; beware of trusting the satirists on Roman Law. Of course, like every educated Roman, they knew a fair amount of law, but their first duty was to the needs of their poetry. If the satire requires an accurate statement of contemporary law, then that is what we shall find. But if inaccuracy makes for a better point, then the satirist will prefer inaccuracy or anachronism every time.

Food in Roman Satire

Nicola A. Hudson

A: The 'Good' Food Guide

1 An introduction to eating 'well'

'You are what you eat'[1] is a well-worn saying, so familiar that it verges on the trite. It is however based on a serious supposition that certain types of individuals and groups behave in a certain way concerning food, according to factors such as economic, social and cultural background. Having pinned down these types we then conclude that anyone from those backgrounds will behave the same way about food and, by the same token, anyone who displays certain food habits will belong to those groups. This crude method of social analysis has led to some gross and glib stereotypes, which among other things provide a rich source of material for humourists and politicians alike. For instance, it is 'common knowledge' that the home counties breakfast on muesli, Northerners consume vast quantities of crisps, elder statesmen run on port and stilton, dieters eke an existence on carrots and lettuce and foreigners eat babies. However, although the universality of these 'truths' is ridiculous, there is still the underlying feeling that the seed of reality lurks somewhere beneath. In fact, in trying to analyse the eating habits of any society, we soon realise that 'typical' behaviour is a term of convenience rather than a verifiable phenomenon. Factors such as age, sex, environment, income and self-perception are part of a complex of considerations that affect what we eat, when, where, why, how and with whom.

The modern world does not have a monopoly on using stereotypical or extraordinary eating habits to paint moral portraits. There are characters in Roman history of whom we know very little apart from their bizarre and excessive attitudes to food. The gourmet Apicius, for example, is said to have committed suicide when he discovered that he was down to his last 10 million sesterces and would therefore not be able to maintain his gastronomic habit.[2] We hear of famous individuals who treated as friends the fish bred in their fishponds for eating; the orator Hortensius wept at the death of his favourite fish and Antonia is said to have given earrings to hers.[3] These foibles were recorded precisely because they were extraordinary.

The Roman satirist also favoured bizarre images of food, extracting symbolic value from them. Juvenal for example devotes a whole satire (*Satire* 4) to a turbot as a symbol of tyrannical behaviour. But although the possible permutations of food as a subject for the entertaining exploration of moral subjects (which is what satire is) are infinite, the Roman verse satirists, although apparently ranging far and wide in imagery, out of satirical necessity restrict their attention to the eating habits of certain people on certain occasions. Therefore, when looking at what the satirists have to say about food, we must also be aware of why they are choosing to discuss the subject in the first place.

For the satirists a useful criterion for judging a person's moral quality was the amount of money and effort he devoted to thinking or talking about food and eating it. The richer you were, the better and more varied the food you could enjoy and the more lavishly you could entertain. So it is not surprising that satirists ridicule selfish gluttons and pretentious hosts. Ridicule is appropriate because, as far as the Roman moral tradition was concerned, the way to the top was properly by pedigree, merit and education. Gastronomy and gourmandry were therefore also morally reprehensible.

Having identified food habits as a suitable subject for satirical treatment the satirist seeks out the moral possibilities of obvious types of food criminal: the glutton, the gourmand and the gastronome. He portrays them as individuals or groups of people who embody the worst aspects of their particular type of 'crime', employing apt and vividly-drawn settings and images. What results is the satirist's technicolour image of bad attitudes to food. The spirit of the genre also dictates that the satirist has to make the maximum impact in the minimum time. Therefore he revitalises clichés and familiar images to suit his purpose. To the same end the satirist invents characters who can be criticised solely for their eating habits. They are extreme versions created to embody all the satiric possibilities of a subject, such as the dinner party, and who must be made to look as if they behave appallingly all the time.

Food was a subject around which had accumulated a formidable set of moral associations—and the Roman verse satirist concerned himself with the moral state of mankind. However, unlike authors who dealt in morals for their own sake, the satirist wrote to entertain his audience, often through a light-hearted re-working of the familiar terms of moral debate. Moral decline at Rome was regarded as an identifiable phenomenon the beginning of which could be assigned to specific factors, such as the growing importance of luxury foods and the arrival in Italy of professional cooks.[4] According to Sallust the following state of affairs had prevailed since Sulla's army returned from Asia bringing with it a taste for gluttony:

> to gratify their palates they scoured land and sea; they slept before they needed sleep; they did not await the coming of hunger or thirst, of cold or of weariness, but all these things their self-indulgence anticipated. (Sall. *Cat.* 13.3)

This moral perspective on food was a popular source of ideas among those who wrote about Rome's moral condition. They used as their standard an idealised version of Rome's rustic past when society had supposedly been self-sufficient and loyalties were due first to country and then to family (as expressed by Lucilius, 1207–8W). Proper eating habits represented one vitally important element in this moral package known as the *mos maiorum*. A good illustration of the values embodied in this code can be found in this extract from Sallust's *Catiline* 9.1–2:

> Good morals were cultivated at home and in the field; there was the greatest harmony and little or no avarice; justice and probity prevailed among them, thanks not so much to laws as to nature . . . They were lavish in their offerings to the gods, frugal in the home, loyal to their friends.

Sallust is here preparing the moral ground for an attack on Catiline. In a similar manner the satirist prepares the case against the nameless glutton and gourmand, often using the clear-cut moral images of the *mos maiorum* which provide an idealised framework for playing the urban present off against the rural past.

But despite the exaggerated flavour of satire, the satirists make their accusations appear reasonable and believable. In particular, they concentrate on the depiction of moral character as revealed in everyday life. For that reason they choose subjects and settings that reflect the familiar and routine aspects of the audience's experience. For example, when discussing the luxurious tastes of the wealthy they frequently use the format of the dinner party, observing a seemingly reasonable order of courses and introducing 'familiar' foods. These foods are often particularly recognisable because they already have an established literary and moral significance.[5] To add to the satirist's air of credibility, descriptions of gastronomic events are 'reported' by sources other than the satirist himself[6] or are described without external comment.

The satirist also derives many of his images from the physical aspects of eating and the experience of a day-to-day food morality. Like the doctor, he considers that physical and spiritual health comes from a balanced and sensible daily regime. The prescription of the proper diet was fundamental to the practice of medicine in the ancient world[7] and in the medical literature it is possible to see the general moral and physical principles of diet which would have been familiar to the audience of satire.

> A healthy man who is both fit and his own master should not feel obliged to follow set rules . . . His lifestyle should provide him with variety: sometimes he ought to be in the country, sometimes in the city, but more often on the farm. He should sail, hunt and rest now and then, but more often take exercise; inactivity weakens the body, work strengthens it; the former brings on old age early, the latter prolongs youth. It is best . . . not to avoid any particular types of food commonly in use; sometimes to attend banquets, at other times to stay away; sometimes to eat more than sufficient and on other occasions eat no more; to eat twice a day rather than once, and always to eat as much as you need as long as you can digest it. (De Med. 1.1.1–2)

These are the words of Celsus, a medical writer of the first half of the first century A.D. Clearly he regards the regulation of eating habits as an important factor in the healthy lifestyle. He would also doubtless approve of the principles that dictate the satirists' philosophical position not only on food but on a multitude of human activities: 'moderation in all things' and 'know thyself'.[8] Eating habits provide a body of exemplary material for illustrating such general moral principles. However, despite their apparently shared adherence to moderate moral principles the satirists do not, unlike Celsus, say that the occasional banquet is acceptable. It is part of the satirist's strategy to invert an exaggerated picture of 'improper' eating habits to achieve an 'ideal' rather than a 'realistic' picture of good attitudes to food. Which means it is up to the morally and literarily attuned reader to spot the exaggeration, symbolism and irony which signal that the descriptions of food in Roman satire are not to be taken quite at face-value.

2 Country life

The satirists seem to agree with Celsus that the healthiest place to be is in the country. More than that, they devote whole poems to playing the rural diet off against the urban.[9] Because the satirist is in the business of persuading us of the attractions of the alternative life and because it is also in his interests to be believable if not truthful, the reader has to be on guard for signs that the satirist is loading his material with images of the past or an idealised present. These signal to the reader that the country life is a convenient antithesis to the wicked life rather than a viable alternative.

The antithesis of town and country gets off the ground in Horace *Sat.* 2.2 where we are treated to the wisdom of an 'extraordinarily sage countryman', Ofellus. He contrasts eating habits in the town with those of the country as an example of the general moral differences that exist in the two ways of life. The climax of the poem is his description of the kind of meal he enjoys both day-to-day and on special occasions.

> As a rule ... on a working day I would never eat any more than a shank of smoked ham and a plate of greens. But if friends arrived whom I hadn't seen in a long time or a neighbour dropped in for a friendly visit on a wet day when there was nothing to do, we used to celebrate, not with fish sent out from town, but a chicken or a kid, followed by dessert—raisins taken down from the rafters with nuts and figs. Then we had drinking games where a failure meant a forfeit, and Ceres, receiving our prayer that she'd rise on the stalk, allowed the wine to smooth away our worried wrinkles. (2.2.116–25)

Ofellus is the only countryman whose diet is presented to us in Horace's satire (the anthropomorphised country mouse in *Sat.* 2.6 is discussed below). Therefore, since we have nothing to compare him with he comes across as a model of sound behaviour who represents all country folk and all country values. However, before using him as a source of information about the lives of the rural population in Italy in the early twenties B.C. it is important to realise that satire was written by and for an urban cultural elite whose interest in the countryside extended as far as country villas which functioned both as working farms and retreats. This urban elite would have been familiar with the potential for idealisation of the Italian countryside through the richness and variety of its wild and domestic products. Moreover, in the didactic literature on farming and medicine we see an enormous variety of herbs, vegetables and other products including artichoke, basil, cheese, chick-peas, cucumber, cumin, fowl, garlic, lettuce, onion, preserves, radish, sesame and turnip, all apparently familiar to the reader and all home-produced.[10] The recognition of this variety does not, however, serve the purpose of the satirist in terms of moral value. He tends to stick to certain types and combinations of foods that took on almost formulaic significance and which had a moral connotation beyond their simply being products of the country. As has already been mentioned, Rome's past was conceptualised as a rustic past. Associated with this commonplace was an idea that the food products of the rustic life had a moral value of their own. Especially prominent in the literary record are the foods of rustic celebration—bacon and vegetables (sometimes cabbage or beans).[11] Against this combination Juvenal judges the frugal dinner described above as a feast:

> This once was a luxurious feast even for our senate; Curius used to put on his modest hearth with his own hands the simple vegetables he had gathered in his little garden, vegetables such as nowadays the dirty chain-gang ditcher in his great shackles who calls to mind the flavour of tripe in the warm café turns up his nose at. It was the custom once upon a time to keep for festivals a side of dried pork hanging from an open rack and on birthdays to serve one's relatives with bacon supplemented by fresh meat if a sacrificial victim gave some. (Juv. 11.77–85)

This particular combination of foods echoes the formulaic version of the basic components of a religious feast as suggested in the *Lex Fannia*, a sumptuary law of 161 B.C. which specified 'expenditure for smoked meat and all green and leguminous vegetables which the earth bears.'[12] The general wording of this law clearly encompasses a possible range of foods beyond the bald bacon and veg. of the *Satires*. The satirists, however, choose to limit themselves to the familiar moral shorthand in order to turn the country diet into a moral symbol of frugality.

The vast majority of Italy's population lived and worked in the country-side, either as part of the workforce of farm owner or landlord, or as masters of their own small-holdings. Rural eating habits would have changed little no matter how widespread Rome's contacts with the world of gastronomic delights became, but, repetitive as the rural diet doubtless was, it could still not be encapsulated in the satirical version of frugal food. Milk and cheese would have been more important to the small farmer than any kind of meat production.[13] Moreover, there would have been variations in diet according to region and local environment and, most importantly, extensive use of wild plants for food. Also, we cannot take for granted the idea that the countryman was content with his diet; the variety available in town might have been attractive, as is suggested by Horace in *Epistles* 1.14.21–5 when he describes his steward hankering for the delights of the town: '. . . it's the brothel and greasy cafe that make you long for the town; and the fact that . . . no tavern is round the corner to serve you drink'. Sadly, satire tells us very little about such people.

Satire takes for granted certain common knowledge among its audience. This is tremendously unhelpful to the modern reader, who often has to rely on the poems themselves as his or her sole source of information. One clue Horace gives us is the non-dietary message which lies beneath the apparent gastronomic detail of the meal. In this meal Ofellus' role is not just to tell us that what he eats is frugal: the satirist is using him to signal a host of moral messages. First he highlights the importance of work and routine, then the important occasions that make it allowable to break that routine. Celebration, however, is not a *carte blanche* to eat as you like—the home-grown chicken, kid and fruit (taken down from the rafters, a vivid image) emphasise the self-sufficiency of the country without saying it in so many words. The drinking games signify friendship, lack of restriction and the piety and fertility of the country. Horace's audience would have been aware of all these connotations and appreciated the feeling Ofellus seems to evoke.

Then there is the nature of the mouthpiece himself, Ofellus. We have a clue that he is perhaps not to be taken at face-value in his name.[14] More than this, he is extraordinarily learned for a countryman, we are told (line 3). He would have to be, as he is quoting the Greek philosopher Epicurus almost word for word! This play on wisdom clearly has a double meaning for Horace and his audience and is a clear signal that this is no real countryman (and no real country meal). The identification with Epicurus comes at the beginning of the Satire where there are close links with Epicurus' *Letter to Menoecus* 130, 'And so plain savours bring us pleasure equal to a luxurious diet, when all pain due to want is removed; and bread and water produce the highest pleasure'.

Ofellus substitutes salt for Epicurus' water. Salt was more powerful as an image to the Roman audience. It was regarded as one of the bare essentials of the civilised life;[15] moreover *sal* (salt) was the satirists' term for wit.[16] Ofellus, like Epicurus, also uses fish as the archetypal luxury food. We see, then, that the literary requirements of satire can prejudice the choice of foods used by the satirists as examples. This does not mean to say that those foods had no place in the Roman diet; but their continued use in literature, especially in satire, which gives an impression of dealing with everyday life, distorts them in the record that survives for us.

The country-style meal has such weight that it can be taken out of its geographical context and used as a moral symbol. In *Satire* 1.6.111–21 Horace describes a country-style meal which he eats alone in the city. It represents a pointed contrast to the city meal which is typically corrupted by the importance of the food and the company. The individual elements of Horace's whole meal have been arranged for maximum moral profit. Horace does not only buy his greens and flour, he asks the price, the implication being that even in the simplest things one can be careful. The parts of the forum he wanders around are the most populous and corrupt, thus emphasising by the contrast the general moral superiority of the country-style meal taking place in the city. Horace's meal, he makes clear, is notable for what it is, by implication, missing: there will be no serving maids, no table-cloth; the wine will be mixed (hence the bowl and the ladle); the only dressing for his food will be oil (not elaborate sauces and seasonings) and his vessels will be local pottery (and not foreign silver). Against this simple framework the luxurious meal can and will be judged. The contrast is very clear-cut—there is no middle ground, no degrees of luxuriousness. And for that reason the extreme frugality of Horace's meal can and must be questioned. After all, it is from just such a dinner that Horace can be seduced by an invitation from Maecenas (*Sat.* 2.7.29– 35—and perhaps from anyone else).

The process of comparing town meal with country meal is repeated in Horace *Sat.* 2.6, in which he retells the fable of the town mouse and the country mouse. The satirist improves on Aesop's version by concentrating on the anthropomorphic joke in the idea of mice holding dinner-parties. The meals of both the country mouse and the town mouse perfectly capture the character of the human equivalents[17] as already described by Horace. The standard vegetables, grapes and bacon of Ofellus, for example, are reflected in the chick-pea, dry berry, oat and bacon fat of the country mouse. The town mouse serves up many courses piled high in baskets (104–5). The essential process and terms of comparison are the same for the human and mouse versions of the urban/rural contrast. Neither is a depiction of hard realism;[18] the symbolism is simply clearer with the more obvious literary controls in the mouse meal.

In his eleventh Satire, lines 65–76, Juvenal describes a country-style meal that he will offer to his friend Persicus:

> From my Tiburtine field will come the fattest kid, tenderest of the whole flock, innocent of grass, and not yet daring to nibble the lowly willow shoots, which has more milk than blood in him; mountain asparagus picked by the bailiff's wife after laying down her spindle; besides these will be some large eggs, warm amid the wisps of hay together with their mothers; and grapes preserved for half the year, as fresh as on the vine, pears from Signia and Syria, in the same baskets fresh-smelling apples rivalling those of Picenum, ones you do not need to fear now that the cold has dried their autumn juice and removed the dangers of unripeness.

As in Horace 2.2 and 2.6, the structure of the piece is directed towards a comparison of city and country habits. Such an obvious borrowing of a satirical idea warns us to watch out for re-use and therefore false weighting of material. What is more, Juvenal has based the framework and some of the detail of his meal on another literary model, Martial *Epigrams* 5.78 and 10.48.[19] In asking the reader to recognise the literary joke here, the satirist invites us to step back from the detail and thus view it less seriously. Eggs, kid, and asparagus are indeed all foods that it would have been possible for Juvenal to produce on his Tiburtine farm.[20] Materially, however, our knowledge of the Roman country diet has not been increased. This becomes clearer when we realise that Persicus has not been invited out to the farm, but is to be entertained within earshot of the Circus Maximus in Rome. The eggs would not have been warm, nor the asparagus fresh-picked. Thus fogging of the truth is revealed as a means to make a vivid image of the important issue, the comparison of city and country.

B: Sin City and its Wages

Ofellus' main criticism of the 'foodie' or glutton is that he is 'swayed by things that do not matter' (Hor. *Sat.* 2.2.25). The country-style meals discussed above (Hor. *Sat.* 2.2, 2.6, Juv. 11) represent by implication 'what *does* matter'. They do not, however, dominate their respective satires, although they are prominently placed, because the bulk of these poems is devoted to an elaborate description of the eating habits of the city which is meant to give as much, if not more, enjoyment as the virtuous contrast. This represents what one might call the titillation factor of satire. In the city/country contrast the satirist sets out a moral discussion that applies generally to all food satire. It shows that a society which places physical wealth, as exemplified in over-spending on food, over spiritual riches has got its moral values upside-down. The Roman satirists use this idea as a basis for comic inversion. They devote whole satires to depicting the food 'villain' at work leaving the morally attuned audience to draw its own conclusions. As we have dealt with the *epitome* of the good dietary life as lived in the country it is now worth looking at how the satirist turns his critical eye towards the city.

1 The Urban Contrast

The archaeological record of urban sites shows that bread, grains, wine and olive oil were much more prominent in the town-dweller's diet than the Roman satirists suggest. Hot food shops (*popinae*) can be found on street after street, perhaps selling the sausages and pastries that among other things tempt Horace's steward (in *Epist.* 1.14) to leave the country.[21]

However, because this type of diet is neither extreme nor strictly relevant to his theme, in the satirist's eyes it is not morally significant or revealing and therefore not prominent in the satires.

The satirist is in the business of implying that there is a whole section of city society identifiable as gourmands who behave similarly and display the same degree of immorality regarding food. This group is described vividly at the beginning of Juvenal's 11th Satire (9–11): 'You see many such, for whom their oft-eluded creditors wait just at the entrance to the market—men whose sole reason for living is their palate'. These characters it seems 'ransack the elements' to satisfy their tastes. Not only that, they will sell off the family silver and ruin their future financial security. The idea of an identifiable sub-group loitering around the market, who can be tracked down at the scene of the crime as it were, is a literary fantasy, the seed of which may already have been sown in Hor. *Epist.* 1.6.57–9: 'let's obey the call of our gullet, going in quest of fish and game, in Gargilius' style. He would send his servants with nets and spears, through the crowded forum'. Such specific geographical settings clearly put the gluttons in an urban context, which is almost automatically associated with luxury and gluttony. The mention of real places in the city makes the satirists' pictures more vivid and therefore more believable, but the pictures themselves are not necessarily realistic. Horace, for instance, is here primarily interested in creating a comic inversion whereby Gargilius 'bags' his dinner not in the country but at the market stall. Juvenal too takes the symbolism of the urban setting for granted when he portrays the subsequent exodus of the city gluttons to the equally corrupt oyster-beds of the seaside resort of Baiae, evidently an extension of the city (11.49): this makes symbolic as well as practical sense and suggests that corruption is in the person and not in the place, thus developing the satirist's theme of self-knowledge.

The full irony of the idea becomes even clearer when we see that the virtuous 'country' dinner, which is Juvenal's offer of 'exile' to Persicus, actually takes place in Rome,[22] implying that he can eat virtuously wherever he is, thus reiterating the point made by Horace in *Sat.* 1.6 (Horace's solitary meal discussed above). Having set an urban scene, Juvenal slowly turns our attention to the country, not as it really is, but as it embodies the moral values of Rome's innocent past (as opposed to contemporary Rome, corrupted by foreigners), and not just any aspect of the past, but its eating habits in particular. Juvenal's own country-style meal leads the way into this comparison: by ancient senatorial standards, he asserts, this would have been a feast. The likes of Curius used to pick their own vegetables (78–9), and meat was only served on special occasions, and fresh meat only if there had been a sacrifice (82–9). The moral virtues of a self-sufficient Republic and its leaders represent *all* of the past just as the exotic catalogue that follows describes *all* of the present. Moreover, the factor that determines that an object be included is its superfluity to the proper reason for dining. That is, it has to be an accessory. In this way the corruption is not simply that of excess. Let us look for example at how Juvenal manages to describe an item of furniture, the couch. First in the past, 'those former times saw tables which were home-produced, made from our own trees: for such use timber was kept if an ancient walnut happened to be blown down by Eurus' (Juv. 11.117–19). Compare this with what Juvenal says about the 'contemporary version', '. . . sustaining the broad slabs of his table is a big ivory leopard, ramping and wide-jawed, made from tusks sent to us from the portal of Syene and by swift Moors and the Indian, darker than the Moor, or tusks too heavy for its head which the beast now sheds in Arabian forest (Juv. 11.122–7). Juvenal has taken his lead from a passage in Martial.[23] But whereas Martial has described a table made up of pieces from different countries, Juvenal has created a sort of 'every table'. Looking at the extract above, it stands to reason that no one piece of ivory can come from all these places simultaneously. What Juvenal has done is to juxtapose the unmanufactured and uncontrived qualities of the homegrown table of the past with a product that encompasses the furthest reaches of Rome's newest and most notoriously extravagant provinces. Syene (Aswan) was regarded as the most southerly place in the Roman Empire[24] and Arabia Petraea[25] had recently been annexed by Trajan. The comment on the degree of darkness of Moorish and Indian skin again emphasises the degree of strangeness to the Roman 'norm'. To enhance the image still further we have been transported briefly to the scene of the elephant's graveyard. Elephants do not shed their tusks, but Juvenal is more worried about the fact that this is an extraordinarily large piece of ivory.

The section of the eleventh Satire that deals with the extravagant accoutrements of dining continues in the same vein. Juvenal is always at pains to stress the depravity, cost, falseness and decadence of foreign luxury items. This affects the items he chooses to describe as well as the terms of description (11.120–3): 'But now dining brings the wealthy man no joy, his turbot and his venison have no taste, his perfume and his roses seem to stink, unless sustaining the broad slabs of his table is a big ivory leopard . . .' The satirist has taken the criteria by which we normally judge the quality of food as a source of irony. He therefore has to choose items which are famous for being highly flavoured or perfumed. Turbot and venison may indeed have been luxury foods, but they are items of food rather than dishes, and have only been given special prominence in the poem because of their usefulness in proving the satirist's point about the wholly spurious nature of gastronomy. Only two examples are required to convey his meaning, but the cumulative effect of this approach has consequences for our overall perception of the variety of Roman diet. Where, for example, are we to find evidence of the complex dishes favoured in Apicius' cookery book? Not in Roman Satire, apparently.

2 Intellectual embarrassment

One of the most effective weapons the satirist has against the wrong-doer is ridicule. Those who take food too seriously are particularly vulnerable to this method of attack. The values implicit in the *mos maiorum* indicate that preparing and eating food did not number among the aspirations of the 'good Roman'. Food was seen as an essential, to be dealt with swiftly and with the minimum of fuss. Those who seek to intellectualise or idolise food, the gourmand and gastronome, are therefore fundamentally flawed. In *Satire* 2.4 Horace presents for our inspection just such an individual, Catius. He, we are told, is rushing away from a lecture to write down 'philosophical' rules, 'which are going to eclipse Pythagoras and the condemned Athenian and Plato's genius' (Hor. *Sat.* 2.4.2–3). These are supposedly Catius' own words as reported by the satirist. His pearls of philosophical wisdom, as we are soon to find out, are precepts for better dining which he delivers without much prompting and in perfect dinner order:[26] 'When serving eggs remember to choose the long variety, for they are superior in flavour to the round, and their whites are whiter; (the shells, you see, are harder and contain a male yolk)' (Hor. *Sat.* 2.4.12–14). Despite the impression that these are Catius' own words, it is easy to detect the controlling hand of the satirist. He has chosen types of 'wisdom' that best reflect the inverse relationship of cookery and more worthy intellectual pursuits. Eggs provide a valid first course for the Roman meal,[27] but they owe their prominent position as the first course of the satiric meal to an Aristotelian connotation which emphasises the proper use of natural science at the expense of the gastronome's spurious version.[28]

The gastronomic information in Horace's satire is designed to support his case in the general moral debate on what does and does not matter. Therefore our attention is drawn towards the relative unimportance Catius attaches to flavour contrasted with his interest in the show-off potential of his 'art'. The gastronomic niceties,[29] factors such as prodigious size, rarity and other natural qualities, are an elaboration of criteria already set down in the Ofellus Satire (2.2).[30] Compare for example what Ofellus has to say about the size of fish:

> Like a fool you admire a three-pound mullet which you have to cut into separate helpings. I know, it's the appearance that attracts you; but then why dislike long bass? Because no doubt in the course of nature bass reached a substantial size whereas mullet are small (Hor. *Sat.* 2.2.33–7)

with Catius' version:

> It's a dreadful mistake to pay three thousand for fish at the market and then to squeeze the sprawling creatures in a narrow dish. (Hor. *Sat.* 2.4.76–7)

We can then look ahead to the final satire of the book and see that Horace has gradually invested in one type of food (fish) special importance as a moral symbol,[31] to the extent that in 2.8 the fish dish provokes the dramatic climax of the piece, 'Then a lamprey arrived, stretched on a dish, with prawns swimming around it' (Hor. *Sat.* 2.8.42–3), and in Juvenal's fourth Satire an enormous turbot becomes the sole focus of attention.

Some pieces of Catius' gastronomic detail are designed to be particularly ridiculous, for example, 'the slippery shellfish begin to swell as the moon waxes (2.4.30). This particular joke is not only laughable for its own sake, but doubly so because it can be traced to the earlier satirist Lucilius (1222–3W).

3 Social disaster

Returning to the extract from Celsus quoted near the beginning of this chapter, one of his other main interests, apart from the setting for the meal, is excess of food in particular at the banquet. Clearly his message is that banquets provide an opportunity to eat (and drink) more than sufficient and that the sensible man will know when he has had enough. While this area of advice broadly overlaps with the concerns of the satirists, the phenomenon of the dinner-party (*cena*) presented the satirist with an altogether different set of moral proposals.

The important feature for the satirist is who is giving the dinner and why. For the satirist the most important consequences of excessive interest in food are concerned with social status. Gastronomic detail is chosen and loaded with imagery that suits his purpose. The main function of the dinner-party satire is to expose the moral character of those in attendance. This is possible because an invitation to dinner served a social purpose and had a place in the Roman social organisation, the importance of which we may find difficult to imagine. Thus we have very little evidence of Romans dining alone. Only once does this happen in Roman verse satire, when Horace dines on the broth and vegetables he would have us believe he shopped for himself (1.6.111–21). A quiet dinner with his philosopher mentor Cornutus is the epitome of bliss for Persius (5.44). Dinner parties were a fact of Roman social life and an important one at that. The dining room, *triclinium*, was one of the most impressively decorated rooms in the Roman house.[32] Those who could afford it had different dining rooms for different seasons.[33] The desire to impress at dinner permeated the classes.[34]

By modern standards the range of status symbols available to a Roman was fairly restricted. A dinner could bring together many of the host's valuable and viewable possessions—silver bowls, fine tables, wall paintings and hangings and expensive food.[35] Food in particular grabs the satirist's attention because unlike the other things it cannot be passed on to future generations, establishing the family as long-lived in its wealth. Because it is so ephemeral, too great an interest in food can be used as a signifier of selfishness and waste. The glutton and the gastronome can be chastised for being impressed by 'things that do not *matter*'.

The satirists present a very clear idea of what dining should be about: the relaxation, freedom and conversation (lubricated by wine) that comes with dining with friends. This is an ideal which depends on the host understanding the proper values of dining and treating his guests accordingly. Unfortunately the satirists never give us a description of a properly conducted dinner other than the idealised rural type. This is the ideal as expressed by Horace in *Sat.* 2.6.65–76:

> Ah, those evenings and dinners. What heaven! My friends and I have our meal at my own fireside. Then after making an offering, I hand the rest to the cheeky servants. Every guest drinks from whatever glass he likes, big or small. We have no silly regulations. One goes for the strong stuff like a hero, another mellows more happily on a milder blend. And so the conversation begins—not about other folks' town and country houses, nor the merits of Grace's dancing; we discuss things which affect us more nearly and one ought to know about: what is the key to happiness, money or moral character? In making friends are our motives idealistic or selfish? What is the nature of goodness and what is its highest form?

This meal bears a striking resemblance to the Greek 'symposium' (drinking party) as described by Plato and Xenophon. Compare Horace's meal for example with the following extract from Plato's *Symposium*:

> When Socrates had taken his place and had dined with the rest, they made libation and sang a chant to the god and so forth, as custom bids, until they began on

the drinking. Then Pausanias opened a conversation in this manner: 'Well, gentlemen, what mode of drinking will suit us best?'. (176 a–b)

The borrowing from literature that has clearly taken place here must detract from the authenticity of this type of meal as a genuine occurrence. Horace wishes to emphasise the proper importance of friendship and conversation and the relative insignificance of eating. The Symposium form presents a clever literary packaging for these values.[36] Moreover the questions that Horace and his like-minded friends apparently discuss are not as innocent as they seem. They raise issues of morality that will be properly discussed in two later food satires—Horace's *Satire* 2.8 and Juvenal's *Satire* 5, in which those who let money be their priority and go through the motions of friendship for the wrong reasons are exposed through their behaviour at dinner.

In Roman Satire some people invite important guests to dinner seeking social advancement (Nasidienus in Hor. *Sat.* 2.8). Others eat well or entertain those lower in the social hierarchy to assert or confirm their own superiority (Virro in Juvenal 5) or attend dinners in the hope of social advancement (Trebius in Juvenal 5). Both of these dinner-party satires depend heavily on the irony of self-delusion. Nasidienus believes himself to be an elegant host, gastronomically inspired; Trebius persuades himself that Virro will be a kind and generous patron. Neither is right and each is ridiculed for the fact. These social relationships and aspirations are described by the satirists using suitable symbols and imagery. To make the images vivid the satirists use polarised terms of description that distort the 'characters' as evidence for the behaviour of real people.

Nasidienus and Virro are hosts at dinner parties. The important thing about a host is that for the duration of the meal he has control over his guests, no matter what the true social relationship between them. The nature of the food served is used by the satirists to reflect the nature of the host and his impressions of what his guests deserve. Thus it is appropriate that Nasidienus is described, ironically, as a wise man and a general,[37] Virro as a king, master or hero[38] and Trebius his poor client as a slave and a monkey.[39]

Although the dinner-party satires of Horace and Juvenal have much in common, they also extract differing types of symbolic and actual meaning from the same foods. This process highlights their development of individual literary voices against a common literary backdrop. Thus a roast boar was commonly regarded as the pièce de resistance of a meal.[40] It had the virtuous overtones of the hunt and celebration meal of Rome's 'good old days'. Nasidienus, however, serves boar at the beginning of the meal to impress his guests, thereby misunderstanding the proper significance of the dish. For him it is much more important that the animal 'was caught in a soft southerly breeze' (7)—his own words as reported by a guest at the meal, Fundanius. Nasidienus' gastronomic fine-tuning is designed to be spurious and ridiculous. Horace chooses the boar as his first example because it has the maximum potential for highlighting extraordinarily gross behaviour on the part of a gourmand. Its value in the satire lies in the fact of it being an unlikely if not unheard-of event, a literary inversion of the norm.

In Juvenal's fifth satire a boar is given qualities that enhance the characterisation of Virro as Trebius' superior. It is served among a 'barrage' of rich meat: 'Before Himself is served a big goose liver, a capon as big as a goose, and a boar, steaming hot, worthy of the steel of blond Meleager (Juv. 5.114–6). The reference to Meleager and the Calydonian boar[41] ironically implies in Virro the excellence of the epic hero. Ironic because Virro's superiority above other men is based on the corrupt standard of wealth and expresses itself in the selfish cruelty dealt out to his long-suffering clients. What is more, the Calydonian boar had already been used by Martial as an image on a number of occasions.[42] Juvenal's re-use of it here adds more to our knowledge of his literary imagination than to the culinary record of Rome. He uses the boar for its connotations of the heroic past. But when such connotations are stripped away, what is left in terms of culinary or gastronomic material? Very often bald and disappointingly unrevealing foods which bear little resemblance to the imaginative mixtures found for example in Apicius or the variety of Columella or even Celsus.

The idea of attacking disparity at dinner was not original to Juvenal in his fifth satire. Both Martial and Pliny[43] describe meals where the host eats better than his guests and Juvenal borrows some of the foods mentioned in the satire from Martial. However, the originality and the thrust of the poem lie in Juvenal's sustained use of the images suggested by certain foods to maximise the social gap between the host Virro and his client-guest Trebius. For this reason many of the foods described are either inedible exaggerations of the Martial standard or already familiar from the moral or satiric food iconography. Trebius receives no version of the meats mentioned above. He has to look on as the patron and his fellow Virros tuck in, and we see that Trebius has been excluded from the convivial high point of the meal. Throughout the rest of the satire, their respective meals are compared course by course. For example, Virro's *lordly* lobster is matched by Trebius' half crab backed into the edge of its plate by an egg;

a lovely embellishment which represents elevated host and cowering guest. Likewise Virro is treated to a mushroom fit for an emperor[44] where Trebius has to make do with a dodgy toadstool. The idea of trying to poison a guest is a literary fantasy, representing the literal extreme of bad food. Therefore the gastronomic qualities of the foods suit the social status of the diners,[45] but, more interestingly, so do the extra terms in which they are described. A final example of this process provides a further comparison with the Horatian treatment of the dinner party. Both Virro and Nasidienus serve apples.

> For the other Virros and for himself Virro will have served fruits whose scent alone would be a feast, like the fruits which grew in the perpetual autumn of the Phaeacians, fruits you could believe were pilfered from the Hesperides. *You* [Trebius] enjoy a rotten apple, like those gnawed on the Embankment by the monkey armed with shield and helmet, who fears the whip and learns to hurl a javelin from a shaggy goat's back. (Juv. 5.149–55)

The helmeted goat rider is a performing monkey. This according to Juvenal represents Trebius' status, with Virro by implication being the Roman equivalent of the organ-grinder.

This is how Fundanius describes Nasidienus' method of serving apples:

> He (Nasidienus) then informed me that the apples were red because they'd been picked by a waning moon. If you wonder what difference that makes you'd better ask the man himself. (Hor. *Sat.* 2.8.31–3)

We know that apples were popular with Romans as a dessert. However, Nasidienus' comment on the phase of the moon at the time of picking is not necessarily representative of the state of gastro-science at Horace's time. Nasidienus' comment is apparently the satirist's idea of a spurious application of a discipline like cosmology entirely irrelevant to the art of cookery.

4 Death by dinner

The death penalty immediately springs to mind as the severest punishment possible in law. The satirists however deal with the infringement and regulation of personal morals and accordingly suggest suicide as the ultimate result of crime against the self and social death as the logical consequence of inflicting injury by gastronomy on others. In Horace *Sat.* 2.2 we are given examples of the ridiculous lengths people go to for a gastronomic experience and the likely consequences of this kind of lifestyle.

> Notice how green they all look as they come away from the 'problem meal'!

Worse still, the body, heavy from yesterday's guzzling, drags down the soul and nails to the earth a particle of the divine spirit.[46] (Hor. *Sat.* 2.2.76–9)

Not only does the glutton's body suffer, so does his purse. A poverty-stricken old age, lack of self-respect, the derision of enemies and, ultimately, suicide are what he has to look forward to, according to Ofellus. The idea of dying from the excesses of gluttony and gastronomy seems slightly inappropriate and ridiculous, since those 'crimes' are concerned with an activity as mundane as eating. Yet the satirist uses the fact of death as the logical consequence of wicked behaviour and the ultimate deterrent in order to hammer his moral point home. In so doing he opens himself up to the charge of going over the top.

The physical effects of over-indulging play a relatively minor part in the satirists' discussion of the consequences of gluttony. They favour one image in particular to encapsulate all the possible physical repercussions—death in the bath. The satirical heritage of this image seems to begin with Horace *Epist.* 1.6.61–2: 'Distended with half-digested food let's go the baths, and ignore all questions of decency'. It reaches its revolting peak in Persius 3.98–103, when the advice of a doctor and a history of palpitations do not come between the glutton and his dinner: 'Bloated with food and queasy in the stomach our friend goes off to his bath, with long sulphurous belches issuing from his throat. As he drinks his wine, a fit of the shakes comes over him, knocking the warm tumbler from his fingers; his bared teeth chatter; suddenly greasy savouries come slithering from loose lips. The sequel is funeral march and candles.' Juvenal weighs in with his own version at 1.143–6. The satirists are playfully making a case for the seriousness of the crime of gluttony. In arguing that there is no other possible result than sudden and violent death we see the processes of literary fantasy and rhetorical exaggeration at their entertaining best.[47]

Conclusion

The important issue for the satirist in the depiction of any area of human activity is the degeneration of moral values and it is his remit to portray them as inverted or, at the very least, perverted. Therefore, although his depictions of Roman eating habits carry the hint or even the claim that they will deliver a verifiable and comprehensive catalogue of Roman eating habits, the Roman verse satirist is primarily interested in the potential of food as moral symbol. As a result he throws into prominence types and combinations of food that already have a moral significance for the audience and which often already have a literary heritage (within and beyond satire). It is for the reader to recognise the imagery attached to the food since it is the imagery which carries the important symbolic message and our clue to unravelling the realistic and unrealistic in the portrayal of food in Roman satire.

'Not "Women in Roman Satire" but 'When Satire writes "Woman" '[1]

John G. W. Henderson

> *You(')r(e) part of the plan | for a new kind of man | to come through*
> Morrison 1984, *A New Kind of Man*

1 If I just . . .

Contemporary feminism makes it impossible to accept what we have been told about Roman Satire or to accept that we know how to get it 'right'. In return, Roman Satire raises pressing questions for (y)our cultural politics.

To take an example—in fact, as you'll realise, much more than an example—what would it mean to you if I collect together and examine the stretches of text in Roman Satire where women figure or views about women are featured? After all, that may very well be what you think —maybe guess, maybe take for granted—I am about to try to do. Perhaps it is. It wouldn't be the first time that that sort of project has been attempted. Perhaps it's a familiar proposition, on the way to being 'traditional'? But if it once may have seemed obviously *sensible*, too—indeed so obviously and so sensible that the point, purpose or relevance of that project wouldn't need, let alone call for, a justification—, I wonder can it seem that way to you right now? *Just* how would you justify it? That is, *if* you would care to try . . .

You could be anticipating here a neat and tidy chapter on the subject. There would be an unclouded horizon, the prospect of an uncluttered introduction and a plunge into the text. Who would need nagging Nonsense: the baggage that is Theory! Those nuisance False Problems of trend, phase & fashion! And—most important of all from where *I*'m sitting —maybe there wouldn't be any special problems for the writer and just sane, just professional, just expert exegesis and just evaluation would do? (Is that *all*? Does that seem enough to you?)

You would, I suppose we could all agree, be contemplating just one more critical study under the aegis of our Humanist Tradition. I have a point or two to make about this before we get to 'Women'.

Because it matters (most of all?) how we get there.

Once it's suggested, I wonder if it isn't just as obvious (to sensible people like you) that this very idea of a 'traditional' criticism has always served precisely to elide the requirement of justification? (Include here in particular the requirement of *self*-justification.) There can't ever have actually been any criticism which was no-more-and-no-less than 'traditional', now can there? Not to belabour the point,[2] to keep on writing exactly the same criticism in 1989 as in — (fill in your favourite date) would be to produce ironically rich writing in at least the one respect that it would be rich in its irony, rich in the irony of itself, rich if and only if being rich in that sort of ironic way is to count as being 'rich'.

In my experience, Roman Satire has been specially attended by a 'no-nonsense' criticism that shelters beneath a claim to be, precisely, 'traditional'. It is half true that this sort of approach 'mimes' some of the main features of the texts it writes about and to that extent it does have a leg to stand on: 'Satire' may be exactly the sort of writing that dispenses with 'justification'. But on the other hand that may well be exactly the reason why 'Satire' is a paradigm of *'bad'* criticism: whereas, on the whole, 'Student Textbooks' don't usually invite—*mean* to invite, I mean—their readers to pick holes in their unargued prejudices—Sorry: judgments—, it could well be a standard feature of 'Satire' that you be expected to ask yourself continuously whether you agree, are supposed to agree, keep catching yourself agreeing, and so on (or whether you *dis*-agree, etc.).

So one of the main suggestions *I* think I am making through this essay is that criticism is and has always been far more *implicated* in its projects, in ways which we are only just beginning to detect, than it has 'traditionally' wished to allow. This applies to literary criticism just as much as it does to other forms, be they social, political, cultural or whatever. More particularly, people used to be very deeply disposed to look for Truths in Graeco-Roman texts, for judgments which are not conditional upon justification, and this is very much what the title 'Classics' once served to specify:[3] I wonder whether you expect or wish to find views you can agree with in Classical Literature. Do you think you should? Do you think this is an important question for your study of the Classical world? *If* it were the case that Roman Satire is 'satirical' in the same sorts of ways as *our* 'Satire' is at least cracked out to be, then would you be looking to agree with or distance yourself from any views you find there? And *just* how, would you suppose, are we to approve or dispute the Theory that Roman satirists wrote or did not write 'satirically'?

Further general observations, now. Surveys, introductions and general accounts of a social-historical kind, whether broadly 'cultural' or more sharply 'literary' in inflection, have relied (too) heavily on the sorts of materials we find in Roman Satire. It's relatively easy—at least in theory —to stop yourself sliding down into simplistic, or at least crassly simplistic, excerption from these texts: the usual term used to 'protect' them from this is 'Literature' ('Poetry' might be over the top, for 'Satire'?). We'll get nowhere if we take 'literary' texts to constitute, or even include, brute 'reportage' of cultural realities. We always want to look for the rhetorical role or function of the detail 'in its context' and we always want to look for the rhetorical target of the overall composition to see what interests it is promoting, what impression it wants to make on whom, and so on, in the context of its culture's discourses, its norms, values, problems, crises . . . But it is always very tempting to get nowhere *fast*: very few books on Roman Life, Roman History or Roman Satire manage for very long at a stretch to resist the temptation to cite a proposition 'culled' (as they say) from one of these texts as if the citation-marks somehow managed of themselves to lend an authority to the view expressed.[4] Indeed many of Classics' most skilful ~~rhetoricians~~ have—let's face it—been employed in dovetailing together, with the minimum of 'comment' to interrupt the flow of quotes, the relevant 'bits' of text and calling the result Roman History or Latin Literature. I think you can see how approaches along these lines relate to the project we're considering on 'Women in Roman Satire'.[5]

One question for this 'traditional' practice of re-citation should always be: if you quote in agreement or in support or as evidence words taken from some 'literary' project, what *else* are you doing beyond eluding the obligation to justify your position? The same goes whenever critics use the notion of 'context' to bound the meanings of details without arguing out how they are managing to delimit this 'context', or whenever critics consider their texts against the background of one or more cultural discourses as if their horizon could possibly be a 'given'. This work of 'framing' is the place where much of the work is being done and—like their nose (that favourite organ of Satire)—it's what everyone overlooks. *If* a critic, for example, writes anything of the logical form 'p, because x *says* p' (where x is a classical writer), you should always ask whether x is just '*saying*' p—Just what could it be *just* to 'say' anything, no-more- no-less?

It seems to me that all this is actually pressed home by Literature in so far as Literature is itself a form of 'criticism'. Indeed one of the main points about 'Satire' is that it may well be offering you a paradigm of 'criticism': it may be the case that Roman Satire is concerned, perhaps above all, to supply a critique of its society, its literature and history: its 'mentality'. It may, instead or as well, be *most* concerned to yield up for criticism its criticism. Does it show you 'criticism' in general, warts and all? It's a red rag and you are the bull? Quite . . . likely. It's a mirror of its dear reader? There are many possibilities (?) All of them call for(th) justification . . . One view of Roman Satire could well be that it's the place in Literature where classical readers (should) find themselves found out by themselves, by their reading. Is this (not) the place where you must wonder how far all just judgments are just prejudices? I like to put it this way: here, before the law of Satire, 'Justification' is most clearly in the dock. And when I do this, for myself I supply two silent witnesses, the hyphens in '*Just-if-ication*'.

Would you join me in agreeing that *if* you wish to be just you'll have to see that justice is *conditional*, for nothing may be *just* 'just'. It can seem to me that this is just what Satire might be there to remind us of. Just there to rub (y)our noses in the world as 'the limitless exemplification of an unstated theory'.[6] *If* you are tempted to suppose that a quote from a Latin author has a better claim to stand as a *just* report on its culture *just* because it *is* a Latin quote, then how does it feel, when you read Satire, to suspect you're identifying yourself with a view that knows itself to be malevolent, phobic, comic capers, just a send-up . . . ? (*If* it does . . .)

There are problems about that neat and tidy project on 'Women in Roman Satire' not least in its very neatness and tidiness. It wants to constitute itself as a separate heading for a separable 'chapter'. And it doesn't want you to find that an issue, it wants you to get on with it, it would rather not (have to) justify itself . . .

Let's take another example which is far more than an example. The decision to devote a chapter in a book on 'Themes in Roman Satire' to 'Women and Sex' could once have seemed a simple enough question of priorities.[7] But what do you think, would it, or would it not, be a distortion of the interests of Roman satirists to include this slice of life as one of half a dozen prime cuts? (For a book of, let's say, exactly 250 pages maximum,—including the Preface—i.e. the 'practical' book for student pockets, that genre which has no room for Theory. Just when you most need

Theory? Or do you *most* need Theory when you're writing for students, for the future?) Or would it be an unfortunate modern distortion? Would it represent an accommodation to contemporary lust for frank (well, fearless if not entirely frank) presentation of raw Roman(n)esses, all that was once subject to 'prudish' repression by modern scholarship (i.e. what used to pass for the Humanist Tradition, the very criticism which our 'traditional' criticism would claim to continue . . .)? In that case, it's not that Romans, or Roman writers, or Roman writers of satire, or the four individuals who penned the classic texts of Roman Satire, or at least these four men in so far as their writing of these poems is concerned—Lucilius, Horace, Persius, Juvenal 'in' their texts—, it's not that *they* were especially bothered to write about 'Women' or 'Sex', perhaps, but rather it's that *we* will be disappointed if this topic or topics is or are not featured in any satisfactory account of this literature? You see how this decision is caught, I would say crucially caught (And very likely undeterminably, too), between a sense of 'Theme' in which we do, and a sense in which we don't, acknowledge that our interests and preoccupations determine our studies of, in this case, Rome? Would you expect one-in-six 'themes' to be One-on-Sex—whether you're studying the Inca or the Dinka? That's *our* problem, not theirs? Shouldn't this issue be given frank—fully frontal—discussion? Doesn't it need all the Theory we can get hold of? Why *this* chapter?

If I just call my chapter 'Women and Sex' and if you do just wonder whether a title like that is supposed to be a routinely descriptive (and so self-justifying) label, or whether it's supposed to give the flavour of Roman 'mentality' (*not* mine, *not* yours, *not* ours), does that mean . . . you are beginning to feel . . . implicated?

That word '*and*' in this title 'Women *and* Sex' is such a contemptibly shy, and at the same time horribly shiny, word, isn't it? It doesn't want you to notice it; interest slides straight off it. What *is* there to say about '*and*'? It would be daft, for instance, to find 'and' and 'or' (or 'and' and '=', for that matter) running themselves together: aren't they opposite numbers? But isn't there—somehow—an obvious strand of 'Women *or* Sex' about the phrase 'Women *and* Sex'? Does it mean 'Women *i.e.* Sex'? I.e. 'Women = Sex'? Do you (have to) see that you (can only) understand 'Women and Sex' as just labelling a category if you are prepared to see the terms as 'a couple', a pair that 'go together' ('Women-an-Sex', 'Women 'n'sex' . . .)? Would you put it on a par with 'Ladies and . . .'? Maybe the title could turn out to be 'satirical', playing on your (eventual) recognition that you were expecting, and/or thought you were supposed to expect, a treatment of 'Women and Sex' to deal with 'Women' as if they are, and/or were, synonymous with 'Sex'. (Try using the copula, like this: 'Women *are* Sex'. Is this the sort of thing—what's maybe hiding 'behind' 'Women *and* Sex'—that you wouldn't want to (have to) justify?) One thing is for sure, is it, that this business of identification of 'Themes' is not simple at all? Rather, it challenges its readers to look for the very justification of its terms and topics which it will decline to provide. How would you negotiate the chapter-heading 'Yeomen and Sex' . . . ? I think that's the obviously sensible, satirical, question to ask about 'Women in Roman Satire'.

2 *Just* . . .

Actually, I'm going to propose that Satire isn't *'about'* women at all. Nor is it about 'Woman', that is to say about 'Images of women'—or Reflections, Representations or what have you—. Rather, I'll treat Satire as one area within the Roman discourse on *gender*. It participates in and contributes to the way Roman culture constructed norms, ideals and fantasies for its people (both) as individuals (and) within its social structures. I shall be developing here a *femmenist* view that on the one hand sees writing along with reading as playing a key role in sorting out and tying together a world for people to live in, and on the other hand finds in gender-differentiation a very fundamental and all-pervasive dimension of the same process of world-building. To find the dynamics of a cultural phenomenon such as Roman Satire we should look hard at the relations between writing and gender at Rome.

3 *If* . . .

But let me stress right now, since it does seem to me to follow from what I have said so far, that no writers on earth—and that includes Roman satirists or classical scholars—can ever simply report or document 'The Position' of women in (any part of any) culture. What do you think? I wonder if you would agree that all writings and readings, ancient or modern, literary and otherwise, are implicated, willy-nilly, in this powerful Truth? It's pretty obvious, once it's spelled out, that this is a 'live' issue (with all the power of being alive plus the danger of electricity). Don't expect, or allow, us to give you 'the facts' here: the finding of labels, an ordered agenda, terminology and conceptual categories is always already inescapably caught up in all-too-preemptive a set of *implicated* views. This goes for what I've been doing. And you . . .

Do find plenty to learn from what critics—and I include Roman

Satirists—have found themselves (not) saying 'about' Roman Women . . .

If we have seen sufficient reason to deny that 'literary' texts such as Roman Satire can just be raided for 'information' and to refuse critical writings the deadpan privilege of supplying 'facts' about Women, then it's time to call into question any half-suggestion you may think I have been making that might encourage you into a 'formalistic' reading of these poems. Critical writings—and educational institutions where they are studied and proliferate—empower Literature to 'inform' its readers in a far more drastically telling sense than the one I've been considering so far. The 'reading' of such texts, whether in the brute sense of buzzing through the texts and translations, or of debating or writing interpretations of their meanings, is a very real way for people (like you) to spend your very real time. Reading Literature is, indeed, what counts as real reading. Whether meditated in private or appreciated in group-monitored scenarios, Literature has (had) a key role in forming us into subjects, individuals in and over against society, giving us ways to have meanings, to absorb, emit and live meanings.[8] Just because a text is 'literary', it isn't absolved from responsibility for the meanings we find it bears. Precisely so: 'Just *exactly* because it *is* "literary" . . .'.[9] To admire, to criticise, to mime, to dissect . . .—these critical activities implicate our selves, our very notions of how to construe a Self. Criticism of Literature is a paradigm place where we negotiate this process and where we make that process the object of our consideration: you should not be too surprised to find that Roman Satire, which casts its gaze across so much of social 'Life', spends so much of its energy delving into literary scenes of production and consumption—and you should wonder if it knows when it does so, that it is in the dock, too, a part of the Literature it criticises.

Noone who studies the culture of a historical society such as Rome can today avoid the realisation that it was always founded not least on the privileging of Man over Woman (as over Slave and Barbarian). The question is whether Classics has always been blind to that fact. Or is this the sort of thing to which you can only be more-and-less than simply 'blind'? Perhaps you can only *play* blind? Actually, I think that it would not be *too* difficult to show that Classics has been, among other things, an important empowering institution in Western patriarchies, catching up, preserving, producing and reproducing 'cultural power under a masculine sign'.[10] It has helped to 'justify' that world-order, perhaps most importantly as itself a 'justification' for it, the operator which needs no justification for itself and which shelters patriarchy from the need for justification, too. No doubt we can see this now largely because, in the disruption of 'traditional' Humanism, Classics has been marginalised so far that its functioning is now available for scrutiny: the veiling of this used to *matter* . . . I wonder if the same can now hold for its revelation?

If we did argue that one of the traditional 'uses' of the study of Rome was to fix in place this blindness to gender-discrimination, the point would not be just to judge and condemn. Rather we should be trying to understand better just how strong a hold on all our experience the hierarchical ordering of man over woman has. This has been one of the chief principles at the heart of the tradition we inherit, the notions of Humanity we act out. Is(n't) it still?

Is Rome so close to us we are still blind to the ways in which the 'humanity' constructed there still constitutes us? 'Western civilisation-*and*-Rome': in very many ways, the world which we inhabit has been articulated round the meaning invested in 'Rome' as a transcendent pattern of Human Destiny. (Remember, this *'and'* might mean 'or' or '=' . . .) Standing for a mature world, a civilisation, precisely, which can face up to the harsh realities of government, the unrelenting duties of the empire, the demanding brutalities of Order, this *is* Rome—'Rome' as *arma uirumque*: so begins the national epic, Virgil's *Aeneid*. Its subject, then, is to be ' "arms"-*and*-"man" ' (do you see that word *'and'* again . . .?). The poem will try to show you all the ways in which *this* 'and' does, and/or does not, mean 'or', or equal '='. Does '(a) man' become '(The) Man' (= 'Man', or '(All *real*) Men'?) in proportion as he 'is' his 'gun'? Should we only heroise the hero in so far as he *is* a 'gun' (*sc.* for the State)? What *are* the relations between these terms—what is a Humanity where 'arms' and 'man' can stand for each other and/or be opposite numbers? What is 'missing' from this picture? For example, what—you might ask (with Virgil)—would 'arms' *minus* 'man' and/or 'man' *minus* 'arms' equal? The *Aeneid* and the culture it tries to speak for, the culture that empowers the epic poem to speak, both revolve around *just* these questions about ?Rome?. Indeed it would not be under-reacting to the *Aeneid* (as I hope you'll discover and re-discover) to say that the culture of Rome is constituted paradigmatically *by* the concerns of that poem. In hammering together a monumental collage of the myriad oppositions, tensions, conflicts and compromises, mediations and bondings between the two initially juxtaposed concepts, 'arms' + 'man', Virgil built 'Rome' *and* 'The Human' for the West, built them round the identification of Society round its Army and round questions about that redoubt. In this context, see if you can see what's missing from the trio 'Roman', 'Human', 'Man'?

'Rome' is the culture where human beings left the tribal hill, hut and valley behind and built a *world* out of the regulation and regimentation of humans. Their City put a principle along the lines that 'A man *is* what a man's gotta do'—namely *fight*—at the service of a World State, matrix of the West. Here at the bottom-line of national ideology, you'll find that the subject who '*is*' is man as male, and is a male male, a manly man. *And that's what he should be.*

Roman educators and Latin writers, are all involved, one way or another, designedly or no, in the engendering of a paradigm voice, to speak for a society organised in terms of this ideology, to call that society into being by the force of the '*reality*' they invest it with. The sublime and so 'depersonalised' epic *bard* Virgil most purely evokes the power of the man's voice which tells its audience (how) to be men, tells them that they can know that this is so, this is the way of things, this is *real*. But the rest of Latin literature plays its part as well in the naturalisation of the human voice as belonging to men, even as it helps weave from a base of naturalised sexualities an overarching hierarchy of gendered values. In the texts of the verse satirists it is particularly easy to hear the voice of Man speak out, realise himself as *The* Self, the one who can speak. All the more stridently, perhaps, because in Satire he is being so 'un-sublime', so 'off-duty', and perhaps, even, so 'unprincipled'. He's *more* of a 'Man' than any epic bard, because, for a start, he's 'personalised' in his writings, he can have a body and a social identity. Satirists give you the model of the citizen saying the way he sees things. As 'his own boss'. This makes him a paradox, but a paradox which still parades the force which gender lends to maleness. It's an important question how far the hexameters that Roman Satire is written in are made to depart from the message of epic. It could be that even as they distort and deform Epic metre and texts they only reinforce epic world view, just turning up the other side of their coin: satirical 'Tails' to epic 'Heads' . . . It could be that Satire's parodic relation to Epic gives us just another empowering of the male voice: the right to be vulgar, funny, informal, trouble; the right to be 'real' *this* way, too . . . (Or is the authorisation of a world view beyond *anything* seen as a 'distortion'? And is 'parody' exactly what scorns efforts to read off a world view?)

4 Just if I . . .

As you'll have realised by now, I am *not* accepting in this essay that 'Woman' *can* be a 'Theme' among themes: a tidy chapter to set alongside others, 'Women' *in* 'Roman Satire'. Instead, I am questioning that *by* writing one—rather an untidy one? I am suggesting that 'Woman' *supplements* the traditional set of topics used to analyse societies and the writings they produce: that is, 'Woman' is (to us) glaringly absent if she's *not* on the list, she shows the set of topics is hopelessly deficient and can't pretend to be a 'set'; and at the same time, once she is brought into the reckoning, 'Woman' makes it all too clear that the other categories are based on her exclusion to the point of her invisibility, as if they could belong to a society, a culture, a very Humanity which could be whole, be themselves, be the totalities which they promise to name, in the absence of 'Woman'. What can't be done is simply to *add* 'Women' to the list . . .

There is no subject, no topic, no category, which is not *fundamentally* affected by the absence of 'Woman'. The opinions and theories which we have inherited are shot through and through with the denial and/or disavowal of this. This absence has been (un)represented throughout our Western civilisation, that is to say those celebrated patches of the history of the West which have aspired to civilisation, as a non-problem: often enough 'Humanity' has claimed to include 'Woman' within itself, as if you could do that without radically re-thinking[11] what is meant by the term 'Humanity' in all the discourses which have made it a master-category. For a start, we *haven't* found(ed) a tradition in which 'Arms and the Man' is discredited as The Question for 'Humanity'. Have we? (For example, 'War on Want' is caught in the *same* alphabet as Airshows, Bombs and Chemicals, our world of Action Men, Armadas and Armageddons.)

I'll look at the four classic Roman satirists, L H P & J: i.e. Lucilius, Horace (esp. *Satires* book 1, poems 2 and 8), Persius & Juvenal (esp. poems 2, 6 and 9). To see their writings as *gendered* projects. These texts cannot simply yield information about Roman Women and they don't merely rehearse the fictional themes of their generic repertoire on the subject: the business of writing and reading them is caught up in the real, 'ideological', work of creating a position from which they can be found intelligible.[12] That's why we are implicated in them. On the principle 'It takes one to know one', texts tell you who you are, who to be, how to read, what is being said, how to view the world. If you can see the world as the texts do, you must (have) internalise(d) a set of ordering principles. Literature is constitutively normative. So if the texts of Roman Satire are there to settle and to un-settle (y)our certainties, if they ask that you see that your judgments are conditional, if they make you ask what (your) views are worth minus justification, they may help you to detect some of the ramifying process by which gender-differentiation has featured in the *engendering* of their thought and language and ours, a process which, it may be, aims to be as vitally invisible to us as the air we breathe.

If you like, 'When Satire writes "Woman" ' is (to be) an invitation to study the way human *'sexuality'* has been structured into rigid categories —'Male/Female', for a start—which then underpin and centre a universe of culturally-constructed *'gender'*,[13] in which Man is built at the discount of Woman into the 'real' human being, the one who knows and speaks his knowledge, the true subject of experience. When Satire writes 'Woman', we watch Men at Work, the work of representing and reinforcing the power of male gender. But maybe Satire performs this, if it does, with a difference, perhaps all the difference in the world—*if* Satire can and does call its own workings as a practice of writing under patriarchy into question, it could make the difference of a world, a world of difference . . .

And *if you just* . . .

5 The fragmeants of Lucilius:

The patriarch of Satire's work reaches us in tatters, a Loeb-volume of isolated verse-long fragments.[14] A 'use' appeared in Antiquity for his lifetime's production of thirty books, one which required that his poems were *not* (to be) read at all. Instead they were cut up, re-sorted according to arbitrary criteria such as the order of the alphabet and copied out to make 'new' texts: scholars hunting for off-beat vocabulary and other way-out *verbalia* looked to just such texts to make their collections with—for L was a 'classic', but one pretty firmly marginalised by the greatness of Augustan culture with its 'higher', more restrained/repressed, writing habits.

'Women in L', then, would involve selection from selection, fragments chosen by me from fragments chosen by the ancient glossographers, via 'editions *of* L' which find a 'new' use for the glossographers' texts, as these are, not read, but cut up, re-sorted and copied out to make anew 'old' texts. Reading a verse 'of L', you're reading a *fragme t* 'of' a glossographer and a *fr.* of an edition of L as well as *f gment* of a Lucilian poem; hence also a *frgmt* of Roman-Republican-through imperial-through-modern-European culture . . .

We should look carefully at the accounts we give of L's Satire and focus in particular on the way that efforts towards 're-construction' deal with the problem that they are bound by the very terms of their enterprise to be a process of *construction*, the creation of a *new* figure from the old materials . . . If we find ourselves celebrating in L the emergence of a new genre and a new personality within the literature of the West *by* producing a (re-)construction along the lines of very *old* stereotypes, we'll be learning something rich as well as ironic. Dealing with *frag ents* always elicits prejudice as it stretches judgment: you might suppose that it's so obvious that in a case such as L we are working flat-out to bridge 'gaps' that we're bound to find it hard to hide our implication in the results. What we do is . . . 'our best'. *That* means we use whatever purchase on L we can get from our evidence and then encourage reason (sweet reason) *and* rhetoric (opportunism) to produce a 'recognisable' figure. The way we do this speaks to our notions of 'humanity': what we'll accept as possible, what we don't wish to face, how we handle limits and norms, ideals and fantasies . . . If all this is true of any interpretation of texts, 'whole' or not, it ought to be plain as the nose on a fragmentary face for L? *Fr gm nts*, then . . .

So the question is how we actually manage to proceed to a positive identification of 'a character like L': an 'exuberant ego'[15] and an 'exuberant genius'[16] who offers 'free-ranging expression of a powerful personality',[17] voices 'his immediate personal experiences and opinions on behaviour and politics'[18] . . . Do you feel you are being directed to *admire* the free-wheeling performance of L as 'archetypal' satirist? I think *I* re-cognise in his writing ('through' the gaps) the transparent experience of a sovereign Self, the Self which reflects back to traditional humanism precisely the 'free, rational, self-determining subject' it is looking for.[19] Is it a coincidence, is it the product of a parallel experience in the onset of megalopolis, is it the construction of 'L' in a mould familiar to us from 19th C. European culture which accounts for the likeness of these sketches: 'Lucilius is a confident, extroverted, outspoken critic who rambles about Rome pointing a finger at whomever and whatever he chooses'[20] and 'The flâneur symbolises the privilege or freedom to move about the public arenas of the city observing but never interacting, consuming the sights through a controlling but rarely acknowledged gaze, directed as much at other people as at the goods for sale'?[21]

Hopping through the *f*a*m*n*s* of L you'd find they 'involve' a grown man with girls and with boys (girls: Collyra, book 21, Cretaea 897, Hymnis, 887–99, 1166–8; boys: Gentius, Macedo, 308–10);[22] when Woman is mentioned it is *as* figure, looks, body (742–3, 1039–40, 1167, 291–4, 567–73 etc.); she is *for* sex, rough sex (1041–4, 302, 361 etc.); *she* comes to him, strips off 'the lot' *et cetera* (897) . . . In the 'Brothel' (*Fornix*, 910–28) you'll find what's *real*: 'Here you will find a firm full body and breasts standing out on a marble-white chest' (923–4): Woman is a body, that is, to assault in fetishised 'bits', her body reassuringly *there*, awaiting *his* touch to make both of them real in all their difference . . . (What *do* people see in Classical statues?)

We are putting together *frgmnts* and closing their gaps: 'When I drink from the same cup, embrace her, lay my lips to her little ones (the scheming jade!)—that is, when I'm lustful' + 'Then she lays side to side and joins breast with breast' + 'and I about to cross legs with legs' (331–4) . . . The effort to 'read' the picture(s) for us represented by these faithful translations shows all too clearly, I imagine. What *is* 'going on'? Can you recover the scene(s)? Perhaps the translation itself calls for translation, calls for a 'reading'? Would you know a 'scheming jade!' if you met/were one? If so, can you know what it's like to be someone who would find themself thinking this exclamation in this sort of context? Is it a kind of 'expletive' or marker of mood, indeed is it (supposed to be) part of '*erotic*' discourse, out to give readers a buzz? Are you *that* reader? Don't run away with the idea that this is a casual example of (rectifiable) translation-error or -fatigue or superannuation. (Mind you, I expect we *could* disentangle the puzzles about the size of her lips, whose 'sides' and 'breasts' and what sort of 'crossing', if we could face it?) The point here is the implication of interpreters, of readers, in the ideology implied by the world view 're-constructed' by their interpretations. Take for example: 'Some of his best invective involves women'.[23] 'Best'?

How do we move from the ?*fragments*? to this: 'Lucilius, the rich landowner who admired horses and women'?[24] Are *we* admiring this? Do you speak this language? Do you recognise this world?

Modern Western discourse produces under banners such as 'liberty, equality and (nb?) fraternity' an ideal of 'a society composed of free, self-possessing *male* individuals'[25]—typified by the 'flâneur'. Maybe you find aristocratic equinity and the hipperotic strange and *other* but don't you recognise all *too* readily the 'phallic self . . . self-contained, powerful . . . gloriously autonomous'[26]?

How do we move from the !*fragments*! to this: 'L incarnates in his phallic brag that perfectly aggressive masculinity of bodily penetration which has been erected by modern scholars into the very condition of a normality in Roman culture'[27]?

Classical scholarship has traced out a sexual normal(e)ness for Rome in which the Ro-man is rogue male who rapes women, anally rapes boys, orally rapes adult males, orally reviles all-comers: nothing simpler, in fact, than '*Romale*'[28] . . . Is this the very core of L's 'down-to-earth, truthful'[29] naturalness? '*FragMENts*'?

Nothing easier than to join other readers—especially the other Roman Satirists, who tell stories of L to tell their own stories *with* 'L', the stories of their own difference within their own conceptions of 'Satire' (Horace

Satires 1.4, 1.10, 2.1, Persius 1.107ff., Juvenal 1.19–21, 147ff.)³⁰—to join them in making myths with the figure 'L'. Since we have just these fragments and since for us the Roman Republic before the maturity of Cicero, whose birth pretty well coincided with L's death, is to all intents and purposes an unknowable world with which later Roman culture made its ideologies, our interpretation of his performances *as* 'L' is largely dreamwork where we conjure for ourselves an 'Archetype' which we can recognise as the '*HuMan*' on *his* way toward, but all too 'free-swinging'³¹ to have yet arrived at, the civilised status claimed by The Classical (i.e. the classical patriarchy) . . .

Does L 'believe in' (any of) the myth(s) of 'L'—all those '*FragMen(*'—? If it were claimed that for none of these *frags*, not one, do you have what you would normally regard as 'context' and that for L's writings as a 'whole' you lack the information you need to place him against a cultural 'background', would that prevent you from 'understanding' him? *Should* it? For example, when we are shown the 'freedom' of L, is this a picture taken (for example) from the pattern-book of patriarchal 'republicanisms'? Or is it a transposition *into* the interpretation of the condition of the interpreter's task, i.e. the 'freedom' from constraints which is opened up by the lack of contextual and cultural materials? Does L feel so 'free' of self-consciousness, fictionality, classical 'writtenness' and so forth because *we* are free to find him so? Is this 'freedom' of ours the licence to re-produce a very predictable composite of recognisable stereotypes? Is *that* what happens when we read *ragments*, read texts as *f   s*, when we read '*frag-meants*'?

6 Humour, Humility, Humanity, Horace:

Satires 1 was Horace's first book. In ten poems he introduces himself and creates a new voice 'for' Satire. He tells how he passed from his freedman father's jurisdiction to be taken up by the (god)father-figure Maecenas, righthandman of Octavian Caesar: not a *son* in a family, but an *amicus*, a 'friend', in an entourage. (It took the great man 9 months of mental gestation before he took up the 'infant' Horace.)³² So as the poetry makes itself known to us, H makes himself known, tells of getting to know Maecenas, gets us to 'know' Maecenas. The poems are examples of H's viewpoint, H is an example of the world being shaped by Maecenas (which is to say by the new Caesar). We are shown through the 10 performances in the book how a new 'L' will see things in the 30's b c e. We 'read' our way into (what was to become) a new Order for the West (as it turns out, thanks to Octavian's social re-birth as 'Augustus'). An education in humanism. You can learn something from this.

H begins with some rough-and-ready 'intellectual' philosophising, with universal 'analysis' of (male) humanity. He will wind down into personal minutiae, a batch of sub-literary anecdote, doodle and joke. Both stages, the 'ideas' and the banter, use a vigorous vulgarity of language, imagery and tone for street cred. This is (to be) a regular, solid citizen speaking out for himself. At the same time, the poetry attacks the instabilities and excesses of its cast of characters to raise itself up to speak to the world of the 'civilised', i.e. the community's powerful in-crowd: *viz.* the circle of Maecenas, and to speak in its name. H sets up his own poems to have their own instabilities and excesses: he devises the mock-humility of a good-humoured self-ironist. Meanwhile the poems preach a moderation which humane humanity (can) live out. What sort of 'satire' is this? A government training scheme? ('Government-training' . . . ?)

Now for 'Women in Horatian Satire'. The voice that speaks out of self-restraint—i.e. both speaks out, *ab-out* self-restraint, and also finds itself (out) speaking *in a spirit of* self-restraint—is a new version of that male Self, 'L the flâneur'. The pop-philosopher who begins the book objectifies Woman as *cunnus*, 'cunt', he takes a whole poem to do just that (1.2). That's how it reads to me: 'men's talk', what men 'know' as males, human(e) or not. All too familiar? We'll see. The chit-chat later in the book personifies the new exemplar for hu*Manism* as '*Priapus*' (1.8). If I translate this as 'Erection', you'll see that I think I know just what 'the vegetation god Priapus' stands for in this poem: a world with a very simple logic, a male logic in which what men say is true because they are men, a world whose meanings are fixed in place by the elaboration of hierarchies around gender based on a bodily imperative of sexuality. If H calls this principle Priapus, 'the prick', feminism labels it '*phallogocentrism*'.[33] It's *the* con-trick of humanism, as of other traditional ideologies? Two performances by H for you to consider, then: (a) Man 'can't resist' women (that's what they both *are*: call this '*nympholepsia*') (b) Man is the imperative of the penis (the reign of the phallus: call this '*satyriasis*'). If this sounds to you suspiciously like (what you might call) '*bonk-n-knob*' (that palindromic pair) more than it does a nice pair of 'Horatian poems', that *could* just be because *you* are caught in the mythology of male desire and can't see beyond the protuberance on your face? Maybe you don't *want* to? *Is* it possible, you should be wondering, to pierce through layers of 'humour', irony and disavowal to find 'behind' them a logic at the centre? And in your opinion do texts have a 'centre' or 'logic', let alone a 'phallus' (I say nothing of a 'penis')?

Does *your* Theory say they don't? Is *that* your Theory? *If* so, *just* how so?

(a) In his first poem H just sermonised on the reason why people wanna be somebody else, i.e. the amassing of riches. ('How big's yours?' At what point do we Yuppies rate our 'heap' a heap?) In 1.2[34] he turns his all-seeing eye from money to sex . . . Something else the 'I' of *men* can have: basic '*property*' . . . He finds 'us' unbalanced and excessive, using up our resources unwisely on the wrong females. He looks into what *you* might (not) like to call 'the mentality of the amorous male'.[35] As he ticks off silly-billies for making such a mess over sex—clowns to the left and jokers to the right—, expensive mistresses and dangerous adulteries, all *that* (*You* know . . .), H and his readers can enjoy looking over 'the field'. *Without* feeling im-plicated. The subject that we could summarise as 'Why all the fuss over females?' is the entrée to a poem-long string of pejorative descriptions. Here they come (again): 'Flute-girls . . . strippers . . . the type that stands in a stinking brothel . . . other men's wives . . . cunts which are dressed in white . . . freedwomen . . . married women . . . Miss Newcome . . . striptease artists and callgirls . . . a married lady or a wench with a cloak . . . Joy . . . a cunt descended from a mighty consul and veiled by a lady's robe . . . girl . . . married women . . . girl . . . a married lady . . . Catia . . . a servant girl . . . 'Not just yet', 'But I need more money', 'If my husband's away'—that kind of girl . . . a girl like that . . . Lady Ilia or Countess Egeria . . . the woman . . . the guilty mrs.' If this is a salacious list, is that the translator living up to the text? (By the way, the word *puella* is behind just one of all these 'girls', the rest are the product of 'English idiom'. 'Miss', 'Lady' and of course 'Countess' are interpretative embellishment, creative translation and . . . a *certain* discourse on gender . . .) How are you going to decide this sort of thing? For example, are you *supposed* to feel degraded by it or is it such a traditional language that you don't even notice?

The most obvious feature of this 'beauty-parade' is that the women are treated as 'bits' 'in bits', object lumps of body: 'feet . . . cunts . . . cunt . . . a straighter leg or a softer thigh . . . O legs ! O arms ! . . . a small bottom, a big nose, a short waist, and huge feet . . . face . . . bad legs or ugly feet . . . from the shoulder down . . . left side' (Nb (i) The 'short *waist*' and '*from the shoulder down*' here both translate the same word *latus*, the one translated as 'side' in L 333 (ii) On the other hand the Latin word specified here as 'side' is the overall term *corpus*, 'body': (i) There are some in-sur-mountable problems in reading ourselves into another culture's sexual discourse: *latus* centres a world of semisupine copulation, a world of 'lateral' sex where noone was 'normally' (supposed to be) 'on top'[36]

(Mind you, *was* there any 'normal' sex? *Is* there? Would it make an erotic, or a satirical scenario?) (ii) Do you see? The woman *is* (just) 'body' and her body *is* 'quintessentially' her *latus*, what a man couples with *his latus*).

You'll also espy through our translation a sort of peepshow of sex-n-text: a male eye/I is titillated by a tissue-tease of clothing plus accessories, that 'obstructed' view which the erotic scene plays as a displaced substitute for the woman, the fetish-structure in which it is the gaze—'now you (men) see 'it', now you don't'—that becomes the place where eroticism is centred and the woman is the alibi (this *might* make a promising characterisation of 'Literature': 'See-through Lingerie. For His Eye Only'? Remember to ask what allows *us* to see any or all of this so readily . . .): 'There are some who refuse to touch any women unless their feet are concealed by a flounce sewn on their dress . . . he fancies cunts which are dressed in white . . . a wench with a cloak . . . a cunt descended from a mighty consul and veiled by a lady's robe . . . she may be decked out in emeralds and snowy pearls . . . the girl with the cloak . . . carries her wares without disguise, showing what she has for sale quite openly; if she possesses a good feature she doesn't parade it and flaunt it while trying to hide her blemishes . . . With a married lady you can't see anything except her face. The rest is covered by her long dress . . . If you're interested in forbidden fruit protected by a wall (and that, I may say, is what drives you crazy) you'll find a host of obstacles . . . a dress reaching to the ankles and on top of that a wrap—hundreds of snags which frustrate you from getting a clear view . . . Her Coan silk allows you to see her virtually naked, there's no chance of concealing bad legs or ugly feet; you can survey her from the shoulder down . . . before you get a look at the goods' . . . Recognise all this? The 'flounce' and the 'wench'? 'Relate' to 'Coan silk'? Sure?

Mirator cunni . . . albi (36), 'He fancies cunts which are dressed in white', says it all, or rather *does* it all. Does(n't) the poet make you see through eyes that see 'white cunt' as 'it', while the translator makes you look at the clothing, the white of the matron's robe that covers and conceals the cunt: what happens when you *explain* a 'turn-on', when interpretation fills in a 'gap' opened up by language? Does it alter the eroticism, for instance from a strange urge—'What colour *cunnus* is 'in' this year?'—to a recognisable syndrome ('What do her panties hide?'. Whatever *exactly* we would put this down to . . .)? H is here crudely summing up the crudity of male objectification of women: he calls the man involved '*Cupiennius*', which must pun on *cupido*, 'lust', and *Ennius*, the name of the great epic poet of the Roman Republic, the bard whose patriarch voice still carried the message of Roman *uirtus*, manliness, when H wrote these poems. (In the very next line, H parodically abuses Cunnius—Sorry! I mean: Ennius—by quoting a sublime/pompous fanfare ('funfare'?) from Ennius on 'correctness/rightness/straightness'. In case you missed the funniness, its 'fanniness' . . .)

In this scene, sex is in a nutshell: *futuo* 'I fuck' (i.e. 'I as male fuck and when I do, female is what I fuck', 127), sexual relations on the model of *impetus*, 'violent assault' (117). Women are objects, 'horseflesh' (86ff.), 'merchandise' (47, 83, 105), they are there to fix the problem of human gender in a civilised world as that of 'sexual choice'.[37] A problem for men of ordering their appetites with a sensible supply of *cunnus*: here women are counters in the fabrication of a world where the men affix the labels, make the meanings stick, say what's what: *metiri possis oculo latus* (103)—the phrase we've met as 'you can survey her from the shoulder down'—more brutally (and do you find less 'sexily'?) says 'you could measure her sex with your eye'. (You could call this '*Eye-balling*', if you didn't mind getting implicated in the sense of humour? It constitutes both the sexual system it describes and also the processes of reading and of translating H, doesn't it?) If it isn't clear yet, try this: 'When a girl like that slips her left side under my right she is Lady Ilia or Countess Egeria;' *do nomen quodlibet illi*, 'I call her what I please' (125f. 'I give to her whatever name gives pleasure' might get us closer—closer to lust, *ad libidinem*?) . . . See?

Has your reading of this poem helped you espy anything wrong with the following (typical) glosses on it: 'The *human* sexual instinct is comic and perfect material for satire, but it needs a socially significant setting to achieve its effect, so prostitutes are without interest, freedwomen are interesting only when men lose fortunes on them, but adultery with matrons never lacks for excitement' . . . 'This is the talk of a bachelor among male friends in a pub. The ethical framework serves a poetic function of unifying a series of portraits that illustrate an important and yet comic area of *human* activity'?[38] The emphases are, of course, mine: but do *you* find these traditional uses of 'human' (un)acceptable? Just *what* allows you (not) to?

You may prefer to read the performance as bluff and matey, 'men's talk' and 'fu-n'. Put the 'call-a-spade-a-bloody-shovel' *machismo* of its language and imagery down to a (rude) 'sense of humour'. And you may find reason to view the poem '*as* a poem'—as an example of the ('Callimachean') poetic where poets made jewels for settings in dung-heaps. 'Literature' need have less than full commitment to the values it presents, perhaps. *Does* 'H' underwrite the position assumed by his 'First Person' in the text? Is the point that the message of civilised self-restraint comes across if you discount 'his' values? Are those values the very object of the poem's 'satire'? How do we find *our* position on this without seeing our sexual, moral, cultural politics implicated, whether we agree, disagree, discount, or whatever? This *may* be the civilised point of the famous 'Horatian irony', that it is civilised to find yourself, like H, caught up in the nexus of judgment/prejudice which articulate(s) social discourse around gender. If you would like a clue that H does 'distance' himself from his 'hero' (and there are many reasons why you might well be wanting one?), maybe H even gives you a clue that he's giving you a clue. Let's see.

When H(e) fantasises his Woman-that-is-all-Women (that traditional wisdom, 'All She-cats are grey in the night' . . .), he puts 'beneath him' her *laeuum . . . corpus*, 'her left side' (125–6). This doesn't just *describe* the positions for the bodies, get them into position, get her where he wants her. It also puts Him 'in the right', makes him a 'lucky' lad. The word *laeuus*, 'left', always promises to carry the connotations 'unfavourable', 'unlucky', even 'baleful', 'pernicious'. And it means 'favourable or unfavourable according to circumstances' where 'omens or portents' are concerned.[39] We can take a hard look at the names he then dreams up, out of all the magical names he could have picked, to see what sort of 'luck' he wishes on himself. You'll recall he said 'When a girl like that slips her left side under my right she is (i) Lady *Ilia* or (ii) Countess *Egeria*; I call her what I please' (125f.) . . . When He shuts his eyes and sees *Ilia*, what does he conjure up? Is it 'the mother of Romulus' (and Remus). Or does he imagine her (as he knew her from Ennius) *as* rape-victim of He-Man Mars at work, rest and play (Fathering the Romans)? Maybe this is the name that comes to Him because it *sounds* lovely, it's the sound *of* 'loveliness'? (You know the sort of thing: 'The feminine falsetto 'i's and the luscious liquid 'l', as in 'L-ily".) Does gender pervade *your* alphabet? . . .) Or is it because it sounds like '*Ilia-s*', a(ny) 'Lady of Troy', too, and so the girl with *Everything*, the complete Graeco-Roman epic heroine? ('A lass. Alas'?) Maybe she sounds just like everyone-and-noone, an omni-compatible termination '*-ilia*'? (Just an Echo, then, as in 'LucIli-a', 'ManIlia', etc.) Almost the same as calling 'her' (*il-l-i*) 'Her'? (An 'Alias' . . .) And maybe just these letters have insisted in His subconscious because '*ilia*' as a common noun spells 'groin' . . . (ii) If you looked down and saw '*Egeria*', would you be plumping for 'a nymph', or for 'the wife and adviser of King Numa' (a Roman would know her from Ennius, who calls her(s) a 'sweet sound')? *Ilia*, then, or *Egeria*? Would you rather be a rapist god of War or a 'married' King (indeed, Law-giver to Rome, no less)? If you weren't fussy which, would that be because you are a snob in lust? ('A 'La(y)dy' or a 'C*untess', either would do' . . .) Or is it a matter of phonetic symmetry, gorgeous *'Egeria'* to complement ebullient *'Ilia'* (just as H brackets Man between the poles *pastillos Rufillus (olet)* and G*argonius hircum*, 'Rufillus smells of sweet cachous, Gargonius of goat', in the sensual line he loved and regurgitated in *Sat.* 1.2.27 = 1.4.92). Or is it *just* that Men don't fancy *any* 'Women', that's just the point, they must 'have' legendary priestesses and fairies? When He opens his eyes, will he find his gold turned to the traditional turd? *Perhaps* H(e) makes himself evoke *'Egeria'* because *'egeri-es'* means 'Excrement'?[40] Is that the twist in the, err, tail the satirist has given his Stud: he chooses for himself an '(un)lucky' (depends what turns you on?) sex *object*, *Ilia/Egeria*—Miss 'Groin-stroke-Dung'? The 'armful' laid on by H for (the males who are) his readers could be as harmful (*laeuus*) to *their* position in the patriarchal politics of the 'Beauty System',[41] where Women are What-Men-see-them-to-be, as . . . (let's say) any armless statue of Venus . . . (*Can* men (not) *hear* 'sexiness'?)

(b) If 1.2 'climaxed' in the sexology of *tentigo* (118), 'tension', the idea that Men will 'burst' under the 'strain' of sexual 'need', and/or it sent up this 'theory', 1.8 thrusts it back upon you, laddies and ladies. Here,[42] the First Person *is* a penis('s). 'Backs to the Wall, Boys!' and 'Run for your "Life", Girls!' It's the talking statuette of Priapus, the disarmingly traditional image of ithyphallic garden-furniture. This 'vegetation god' stands up and sticks up for the divine principle that male sexuality is simple. Here he *is* the seed-label which reads 'Erection!', statuesque and symbolic. Priapus may be a whole android, but he *is* his penis—his and every penis, for the 'real' penis is erect, this is the 'reality' of Manhood. His figure images this over and again: 'the weapon in my hand', 'the red stake projecting obscenely from my crotch', 'the reed stuck in my head' (4–7). Equate the pole/penis with the warrior's *right*, i.e. combatant, hand, what makes a male manly; the reed sticks straight up to double as (i) crown-spike to top off the erect head of the erect image and (ii) snare tipped with goo to catch any under-impressed or unwary birds. His job is to keep Maecenas' garden rosy. He rapes anything that moves: wild nature, human, subhuman . . . or female (thieves: 3f., 17; birds: 3, 6f.; critters: 17f. (*ferae*); females: 19f.). He is a 'terror' (4). This *is* going to be 'fun', that's the promise of Priapus . . .

When H plays Priapus, he guards the gardens where cultivated friends of Maecenas (such as H) can dream up civilised poems (such as this one). Here the poet can live his poetic life, cut a (funny wooden) figure for himSelf. As H does so, Priapus risks having to play H. And the name H always wears in his satirical poetry is *'Flaccus'*, which in this sort of context is always going to mean 'soft, impotent, unManned' . . . The Priapus of H's satire may be less of a 'terror' than he usually is? (Will he go off half-cocked?) The civilised satirist will 'stand up' for himself rather less than, say, the unrestrained L did? Before deciding this too soon, ask the question, isn't Priapus the same as any stand-up comedian, unmanning *everything* he attacks, *including* himself? If a Bernard Manning turns to talk about himself, he's bound to send himself up. (We could call this '*Self-deprication*', if you like?) But we all know (do we not?) that the Joker doesn't come off the worse for this: the bigger the Joke he makes of himself, the better he is at his job. He's a traditional figure, he's the alibi which lets Men badmouth *everything*. 'Funnily enough', as you might put it, H/Priapus is here to turn on two women. Not 'Lady Ilia and Countess Egeria', this time, but 'Canidia' and her sidekick 'Big Sagana', not the fantasy projections of male lust but two working women—what you might join in victimising by agreeing to call them 'a pair of silly old hags'.⁴³ Without feeling in the least implicated . . . Until, that is, you notice that 'hags' puns here on the colloquial phrase 'silly old *bags*', and you see that black magic haunts this poem still: calling Canidia 'a witch' might not seem a terribly civilised or 'funny' thing to do, whereas none of us are going to recognise 'hag' as a descriptive category and 'old bags' is an obviously vulgar jocularity that none of us *sensible* people could mistake for our own cultivated values. So it's O.K. for us to call 'em 'hags'. Is *that* it?

Canidia comes with Sagana to Maecenas' garden. 'Bitchy', along with 'Witchy' (know a woman from the company she keeps: *sagana* means 'a wise woman').

'She is described in horrifying and ludicrous terms that are appropriate to any witch'. That's *one* version. What does she come *for*? Which answer would you like: gathering nuts in May, 'gathering bones and deadly plants' (21); to make Priapus 'stand in terror' (45) before his eventual 'triumphant if involuntary revenge'; to give him a funny story (Worzel Gummidge in Latin?); to indulge in traditional ridicule of women . . . ?

Here's another 'description'. Canidia comes to the garden to make a pair of wax dolls: 'The larger doll represents Canidia, the smaller her lover, who is being punished for his lack of devotion'. (Though the text doesn't say so: 'lover' is supplied by the translator.) So Canidia comes to the garden *because she is a Woman in Love*. She acts out a fantasy scene in private. Where no *man* could see her. She and her friend can make no impact on the real world they come from. They make-believe, like powerless children, with dolls and moonshine. They get their way, pull the strings, work triumphant and voluntary revenge, the only way they can. So a Man is to blame for Canidia's visit? (Though the text doesn't say so: '*his*' in the phrase 'his lack of devotion' is supplied by the translator.) But perhaps, too/ instead, it's because love makes *all* humans feel desperate and impotent —Maybe *that*'s the (black) magic of love?—Perhaps, again, it's because it's a Man's World? . . .

What do you think? Does the poem itself represent, stand for and stage the 'Man's World'? Doesn't it? I think we can make out Canidia's rites through the moonlight across the rich man's lawns on the common land where the poor once buried their dead, even though the text doesn't make 'the details' 'exactly' 'clear'. See, the witches represent disorder: they collect 'anti-matter', dead 'bones' and 'deadly' living 'plants'; body veiled by a long 'robe', legs revealed by its being 'tucked up'; 'black' clothing, faces' 'pallor'; from top-to-toe (so totally) liberated—from 'barefoot' to 'hair streaming free' (so knotless, beyond all restraint, by self- or otherwise)—. Their rites act out a return to the primitive: the voice a pre-verbal 'shrieking'; 'their nails scrape away' a trench, as if before the invention of tools; they tear a lamb 'to pieces with their teeth', doing without kitchen and kitchen-knives; they confuse life with death, 'summoning up the spirits' but using wax dolls to punish their victim (rival? beloved? Anyway, soon to be the 'Ex'!) with what looks like 'a slave's death'; as they pray/curse (let's say: 'anti-pray'?), there swarm round them their animal avatars, the creepy-crawlies ('snakes' and maybe more . . .) 'and hell-hounds' (feminine hounds, actually, so bitches all . . . 'Canidia' must, for all her long 'a', have *something* to do with '*canis*', 'dog/bitch'[44]) . . .

What lets us read these rites through the meagre 'details' given by the text? How do we fill the gaps in these 'fragments'? They feel 'traditional', presumably. That is, they belong to a tradition which we still 'recognise'? We 'know' about witches. We read about them in books, for a start. (For many of us, it is *the* start of reading: the witch has been one of the few female figures in children's books who ever manages to *do* anything—even if usually someone does exact 'triumphant revenge' over her . . .) Witches represent traditional 'opinions' about Women. It should be clear from reading a fantasy-fiction such as H's—'The Talking Knob has spoken', indeed!—that witches have a part to play in the way that women have been denied real power in the world: *some* women must be treated as if they really *could* threaten Men, precisely so they can be put back 'in their place'. So the witches are a 'terror' to Priapus the 'terror' but he gets the last laugh on them. (*He* says) The women's 'fly-away' (so unleashed) locks will turn out to have been 'wig' and the 'bite' that tore apart the living lamb must in the end become 'false teeth' that fall out (these are the 'bit-ches' who 'buried a wolf's *beard*' (a *wolf*'s, get it?) 'along with the *fang* of a spotted snake' as they burned their dolly, 'as a precaution against counter-spells', i.e. so the biters wouldn't be bitten back). Witches *quae uersant . . . humanos animos* (19f.), 'plaguing the souls of men', are supposed to use *carmina*, 'songs/spells' and *uenena*, 'love-drug/poisons' to do this. If you just stop for a moment, you'll see that H is using Priapus to use his 'verses' to turn the tables on Canidia. This poem is itself a *carmen*, 'poem', full of *uenenum*, the 'poison' of a satirist's writing and of a comedian's joke and of the foiling of a 'love-drug' in the story. The *telling* of the story *does* metamorphose the frightening witches into 'a pair of silly old hags'. The male voice uses its monopoly of language to do so. Priapus punctures his 'terror' with crude toilet-talk: 'the droppings of crows' (Birdshit, to you!), 'piss and shit' (37–9). Then his body finds *its* voice and the god masters Woman with a triumphant 'fart'. A sort of comic version of Jupiter's thunderbolt. In the end, the women run in fear from Man. Along with the dentures and hairpiece, their 'herbs and enchanted love-knots fell off their arms'. One peep at the *real* women, minus their accessories, and 'If only you'd seen it! You'd have laughed and cheered!' Do you see how many ways this story shows us that 'Men are real. Women are "made up" '45?

All the same, the victorious 'fart' which let the Man-at-arms disarm the women, did, so the translator tells us, cost Priapus dear: namely one 'large crack in its posterior'. He has told the story at his own expense, as well as Canidia's. Presumably, don't you think, a self-respecting Priapus would have had 'Lady Ilia' and 'Countess Egeria', 'lovely Lola and ga-ga Garbo', drop by his patch and would have impaled the pair of them before ejec(ula)ting them from his beds (simultaneously? A divine miracle . . .)? It's a question whether the Priapus-figure's new improved action is or is not a demonstration that 'restrained' civilisation-à-la-H sees 'humanity' any differently than the old aggro of 'L'. Is(n't) it the case that to speak of 'witches'—let alone 'hags'—is always already to identify *humanos animos* with 'the souls of *men*'? (To identify them as closely as those two Latin words jingle together out loud—Remember, by the way, that 'Flaccus' is 'Mr. Softie' in Latin. *Animi* cover 'minds, hearts, mettle, courage'. Witches should turn H over like icecream in a cauldron.)

We can realise that the poem is put to 'higher' use. Priapus *is* an occasion to picture the processes of purging and re-construction that the Caesarian order is (supposed) to spell for Rome. The gardens of Maecenas are a start towards a new 'tomorrow', putting 'behind' them the putrid, poisonous old 'then'. This smallest poem in its book can carry its biggest message . . . And it's witty. We can appreciate H as a 'nice' man, who pulls back from the aggressive voice of his street sermons (1.1–3), as he yields to his own lessons of polite self-restraint, to give us a disarming raconteur who tells us funny stories that (irony of ironies) imply so much . . . Still, this 'new Man' waves it right in your face, does(n't) he, that 'traditional humanism' is built—all the more solidly for its humour and humility—round the 'Iron' Law of phallogocentrism? Priapus has-and-is the erect phallus, he owns the words and runs the logic, he is the heart and soul of the garden, the centrepiece. When (he makes) the women come and make him their *testis*, (36, 44) 'witness', he is making the traditional pun on *testis*, 'testicle' (appropriately enough, a *pair* of puns). What he can swear (as 'witness') that he saw ('With my own eyes I saw . . .', 23, is a courtroom formula) is what he wants *you* to see, for *cum magno risuque iocoque uideres*, 'you'd have seen it with a big big laugh, such fun', as we could translate it. (The last words of the poem, these. Its 'last laugh'.) Even if you (as male, it goes without saying) don't use your phallus, even if you're 'involuntarily' reduced to a 'fart', the victim will still, traditionally, be Woman and the 'triumphant revenge' will be *His*. Because your testicles testify that you are a Man, what you witness is real, what you see is as you see it. You can *always* make it happen, because your voice has owned language, you're the one that gives everything its name. Especially 'humanity'.

Does(n't) H make all this look silly? Ol' Blue Eyes Priapus did it his way. 'If you'd seen it', *just where would the joke be?*

7 Philosophy Saves Our Souls: some Advice from Persius

In his second book of satires,[46] H falls still farther back from using the aggressive voice of a virile Satirist. Instead he presents a series of all-too-knowing characters who demonstrate the principle discovered in book 1, that you must say your philosophy for your Self, what it all means depends on who voices what, what you learn from your teachers depends on the lesson *you* read them as teaching. In particular, the wise men who (think they) know the answers, above all the 'philosophers', have impressed their answers on a range of characters who try to impress them on H. And so on us. We ask throughout whether the *poet* is also, or instead, the 'wise man' for us. Our guru. We are caught, then, in the civilising contemplation of an enigma. H is, of course, throughout, the one who is trying to impress his views on us. His characters are, in a way, his (character(s)). Can anyone teach teaching? Whether or not the teacher thinks he knows any answers?

The material of *Satires* 2 features various of the ways in which men may (fail to) regulate the living of their lives. In H's *Epistles*,[47] the range is just as wide but the focus has come (back) down to spotlight H. We 'read' H in the broad range of his social, civic, personal relationships, all of them bringing out different sets of ideas, inflections, discourses, in a batch of letters from which you have to get to know the missing correspondents so that you can read H *and* the correspondents from the 'replies' he gives to them. The reader plays the whole cast of (male) social roles from slave to Emperor and at the same time gets to know the writer's 'reading' of those roles. His writings *are* those readings, those readings tell you how H sees things, and that is who H *is*.

If it occurs to you that women have next to no place in these texts, this would not, of course, be true of *gender*. The poems are pervaded by representations of huManity in a Man's World. As H turns to the philosophical lectures preached 'to' him in *Satires* 2, as he reaches in *Epistles* 1 for the philosophy by which to live, representing to us in the process the philosophy he *is* living by, namely a life lived in the search for a philosophy, his concerns progressively address themselves to the business of 'opinions' and 'theorising'. 'Women and Sex' drop away as preoccupations.

They are the crass 'first' mistakes that philosophy must expel from its aspiring gaze . . .

With P,[48] the satirist takes up from here. His satirist doesn't walk round the city, he doesn't picture for us his idea of convenience-copulation and doesn't (ex)pose his Erection only to fart his way out of trouble. 'P' renounces his body, barely retains his voice. He doesn't look for street cred. You wouldn't confuse him with a 'Man', he's neither 'One of the Boys' nor 'Man-about-Town'. With him Satire has gone 'philosophical', his writings are a struggle for *uirtus*, 'Virtue'—in a sense which you are *not* to confuse with 'manliness'-as-'virility', '*Maliness*'. The First Person in P is an adolescent male struggling to follow his lessons. There's no question of 'Life in the Brothel' here, no Treaties, anecdotes, biography, Maecenas, friendship, 'fun'. 'P' sees himSelf lapsing from the Stoic lessons he learned, was supposed to learn, in school and disappointing his mentor-guru Cornutus (5, esp. 36f.). Like Seneca and other citizens of the C 1st c e absolutist court of the Roman Empire, P turns 'inside' to look for an authentic Self in 'mind's recesses undefiled' (2.73), to take the 'climb-down into himself' (4.23) that is to constitute (true) 'freedom' (5 *passim*, esp. 36f.).[49] He eschews street cred. and common sense, he writes of(f) his Society: '*That's pretty!* Pretty, that? Is Romulus a poof?' (1.87) They are all 'Trojan women', 'huge Tituses are seen to thrill as poems enter their loins and vibrant verses tickle the inmost parts'; to 'our heroes'—'your smoothie Trossulus' and co.—Virgil's *'Arms and the man*—what's that but froth and fatty crust'? . . . (1.4, 20, 36, 82, 96). The body becomes 'this guilty pulp' (2.63): rowing, the bullworker, jogging, these are *not* the answer! P turns away from Maleness, revolted by Erection-Aggression—'What morals! Weeding penis and loin's secrets! Exhibiting your drooping onions to the public!' (4.35f.).[50] Philosophy shows you that the traditional paradigms of Manliness, the 'Rambo' RoMen, are sick, sicker than they know—'Some he-goat of the clan Centurion' (3.77), 'Our highly muscular young' . . . (3.86): 'Say this among the varicose centurions and huge PulfEnnius bursts into a crass guffaw, bidding for a hundred Greeks a clipped hundred-*as*-piece' (5.189f.) . . .

'Women and Sex' in this view look like this: 'so that this wild grandson of yours . . . when the temperamental vein throbs in his roving groin can impiss some noble bag' (6.71f.). 'Sex' looks like this: *si facis in penem quidquid tibi uenit*' (4.48), 'If you do whatever comes to penis' . . . And yet. The 'I' who shows you this vicious world shows you himSelf as nothing to write home about: he skipped off school as a boy and now snores his student way through last night's hangover to mid-morning. The voices in his head tell him he's work to do, but . . . (3.44f., 1ff.). On the one hand this First Person has taken the first step toward Virtue in recognising his vice. The strength of his self-criticism indicates the strength of his chances of health. So does (y)ours? On the other hand, what credentials has a mess like this to go preaching Virtue? Doesn't the world know that his vision of a sick world is a sick vision? From whose v(o)ice do you take *'Ad-vice'*? The reading of P gets implicated in a struggle to weigh up the voices which speak their Theory and their Opinions, their wisdoms and their contortions. As the Satirist turns inside, his writing stops imitating a sort of 'conversation'—'quasi-spoken' in *Sermones* (The *Satires*), 'written' in *Epistles*—and instead his 'voice' crumbles and threatens to break up so that you can't simply take the chunks of language to be 'unified' or 'centred' by their origination from one Self. (P 3 is the classic performance.) As P shifts in and out of First-, Second- and Third-Person pieces of language, 'gaps' open up in the poetry and reading them becomes a process of filling these in, with '(re-)constructions' which sort out which 'bits' are supposed to ring true and which are sent up, (self-)satirised. If we were reading from fragments of text to 'find' the author 'L', and then we read through 'fragments' of social discourse to read 'H' as hub of his world, now we tack together the 'fragmented' voices inside P's mind to assemble a soliloquy that possesses as much or as little coherence or as much implosion as our notions of human mentality suggest. Just which bits *does* 'P' (wish to) 'authorise'? To ask this question may be a civilised education (for us as for P)? Is *that* it?

If I just mention 'Socrates' (who 'runs' P 4), you'll perhaps see that the 'philosophical' scene in P may presuppose traditional opinions about education, and so about civilisation? No place, precisely, for Women in that 'Platonic' scene where you boys have talked with the Professors and they've all liked your looks ... Nevertheless, in her absence, here is a biopolitics saturated with *gender*, the regulation of living according to a system articulated in terms of maleness-and/as-manliness. A whole set of regulations, from stigmatisation to idealisation. The question will be: Can the 'abstractness' of *'Virtus'* survive a Satirist's representation of its all-too-concrete aspirant? Does P's voice jettison mundane criteria for judging him to be a 'Man'? Or does 'P' retain those atavistic qualifications still *because* his voice gives the world 'a beating'? What does P lose if he loses his voice(s)? Does it take virility to find Virtue? Will a *real* 'new Man' renounce that old virility? Should we recognise a familiar story here: 'Modernity is characterised ... by the withdrawal of the person into the private recesses of the inner self ...—the locus decreed by the ideology of contemporary sexual imperialism'[51]? Does (or did) such an 'alienated' modernity altogether bypass *Women*? Whose 'problem' is it (supposed to be)? *Which* 'humanity'?

8 *Juvenal the ShowMan puts on a show*

J[52] begins by giving readers to understand that he performs as an 'alternative' declamatory reciter who speaks 'for' an audience used to the cultural game in imperial Rome of virtuoso rhetoric for light entertainment (1.1ff.). Can we read from this an invitation to register his Satire as 'the *portrayal* of indignation'?[53] This would then be no personal statement, let alone Quest, but a series of performances from a 'Bullshitter'. *Sensible* readers (like you) would realise that the values spoken by this orator are screened by a multi-layered alibi—the declamation isn't 'serious', its work of 'impersonation' is just another exercise in the schooling of RoMen citizens; furthermore, this is a poetic simulation, a literary variant of the 'declamation' which, in fact, *pretends* to be a declamation, wants you to admire, not to miss, this pretence; and besides, this text marginalises its speaker so *obviously* as bigoted, unstable, bathetic and so froth ...

A *really* sensible reaction to this could be to read through this web of disavowals and expect ... a volley of crudities, all those crudities which *for real* you would want to find unacceptable, the ones which you know make up and support standard, 'normal', attitudes? (You could be reminded of the many jollities of our 'popular press'.) As you play along with this so that you can pretend it's just vulgarity, that's all, ask whether this isn't a 'civilised' game designed to secure a public arena for crudity: as if that is just one more way to be civilised? Is(n't) it?

The point of (Self-)Satire in J will still, in any case, be that you are invited to find *some* of the views untenable, crazy, daft . . .—But which ones? *That*'s where you must get implicated, for not every single item in the string of remarks is going to be disowned by any reader. If you draw a line, just where do *you* draw it? When the writer cancels *his* authorisation of his writings, it's left to you to plot your own way through them. And to wonder what motives you could have for playing at all. Still expecting lessons?

You'll find J satirises *Men*, (a) ventriloquising a 'Woman' (J 2) and (c) consorting with a 'Superstud' (J 9). And (b), as well as composing *the* '*pornotopia*' in Latin (J 6), J makes the world of his poetry turn around an insatiably aggressive and irresistible lust . . . the lust *of* (not 'for') women (*passim*). This *must* be just 'fun', because it can *only* be a fantasy . . . Just what will *you* be looking for(ward to)? If you're already deciding 'he *CANNOT* be serious', does that just mean you're already caught up in J's disavowals, you're going to feel free, free to enjoy watching the fur fly: no more implicated than . . . the next man . . . ?

(a) J 2^{54} begins with a rant against pathics (1–35): no place for women here! The poem swells through scenes of 'gender-bending' T(rans)-V(estite) outrage from the sexy transparence of the lawyer Creticus' gown (66–83) through a chorusline of male devotees of the women's goddess, the Bona Dea (84–116) to the climax of the aristocrat jet-setter Gracchus' wedding-scene (117–42): *he*'s the bride. From there on (you may find yourself deciding), anticlimax: the bathetic claim that Gracchus' performance as gladiator was a still worse outrage (143–8), which serves as a 'transition' to the finale, a tirade on the global corruption of the Roman tradition of soldierly *mores* (149–70). *If* you so decide, of course, you'll have to justify *your* perspective *against* the view presented by 'J' . . . Some people, some of them Romans, some of us in some cases, may feel that private eccentricities *are* just smut but public degradation really *is* a national disaster. And then, you *may* feel that J's 'reporting' on the wedding is all-too-obviously lurid and lip-smacking (well, *you* obviously enjoyed it . . .), whereas his descant on 'National Service' just accents literary parody? . . .

Satire in J 2 reverts to the old 'men's talk' and its crudities: sexual invective, genital puns, a 'nostalgia' for the loss of traditional values. 'J' is a Male out to insist on a gulf between Men-like-himself and any dubious *'homines'*—'civilised' human beings, decadent weaklings, or whatever—. Moralists 'sham the Curii' but 'live like Bacchanals' (3). Philosophers are 'solemn perverts . . . Socratic cinaedi . . . those who assail such things in the phrase of Hercules, and having talked on virtue' (*Virtus*, remember, spells 'manliness') 'wag their haunches' (9f., 19f. You can't fault the translation 'cinaedi', now can you?). 'These bogus Scauri'! (35). 'First consider men:' (*uiros*) 'Great the concord among the soft' (*molles*, 45f.; *mulier*, 'woman', was linked with this 'softness' as its incarnation . . .). 'Mirrors in the baggage of civil war!' (103) 'It takes a supreme general to slay Galba and prink the skin; a supreme patriot's staunchness to affect the Palace throne on the field of Bebriacum and with the fingers spread compressed dough over the face' (104f. 'To prink'? To . . . *do what?*) . . . At the end we learn that the Empire's secret weapon is that royal hostages transmit back home perverted Roman *mores*: *hic fiunt homines* (167. 'Here they are made adult', but more pointedly, 'here they become *human beings*, i.e. civilised, human(e)'). But as 'J' frames a world—shows you the world of 'Rome' and 'the West' *is* framed—round gender-difference, remember that he first of all slams the pathics who hide their betrayal of manhood behind a 'front' of moralistic preaching before he turns on his men in frocks: The question presses, (just how) can *his own* sermonising escape the net? And, there again, *if* it does, how does he get to play fly on the wall? J hardly has the excuse of the doctor and his (satirical?) sense of humour for witnessing this private scene: 'Hirsute limbs and hard bristle along the arms . . . but from a hole that's smooth the chuckling doctor cuts the tumid piles' (12f. Still, why *do* people go in for Medicine?). How are we to agree the point at which he starts guessing, reproduces the twisted fancies produced in his brain, betrays the pleasure he takes in the verbal display of disgust? Where does the pleasure of reading originate? Is(n't) this for Men Only?

J puts up a woman called Laronia to declaim 'the obvious truth' against the hypocrisies of pathic moralists (36–64). He uses *her* to defrock these men. As she does so, she bridges to the next scene of men wearing clothes to their drag weddings (65–142) by telling us of wifely men weaving cloth (53–7). Does it take a woman to know a woman, to know men as men cannot know themselves, to 'understand' TV? Or is Laronia the Satirist-in-drag, bound to travesty women just as 'J' travesties men, just one more way for J to devise self-satire: 'You will not find any instance as detestable in our own sex. Flora does not lick Cluvia, nor Catulla Mevia . . . Do we' (Wait for it!) 'argue cases, of civil law do we have knowledge, or stir with any noise those courts of yours? A few of us are' (Here comes the crunch!) 'wrestlers, a few eat aitchbone steaks' (49f., 51f.). Is this supposed to be the 'best' that can be said 'for' women? Laronia's complaint is that 'The censorship condones the crows, harries the doves' (63): the kettle (for once) calls the pot as black as the pot (always) calls the kettle. So it's 'ducks-and-drakes'. Does the introduction to Satire of 'a woman's point of view' amount to no more than . . . a transitional device? Is it just more 'fun' for the boys? Best to see 'Laronia' as marking another absence of Woman? (A suture . . . ? Remember those piles . . .)

  (b) Were we to run through J's Satires looking for it, we would find his First Person elaborating the traditional crudities of Adultery-Invective while letting slip a reassuring supply of the usual sentimentalities of 'normal' exogamous and familial ideology. This is the very way that the 'epic' (cum 'tragedy') of J 6⁵⁵ begins, looking to naturalise these ideals by planting them firmly at the origins of humanity 'In the reign of Saturn', before the interference of culture: '. . . when a . . . cave provided men with . . . homes and a fire, a lars, and cattle', '. . . when a . . . wife bestrewed her . . . bed with . . . straw, and hides of . . . beasts', 'bearing . . . babes', and there with her was 'her . . . spouse' (1–7, 9f. Actually there's no word for 'men' here in the Latin). Even as he provides this nostalgic picture of HuManity in its natural habitat as yardstick to beat 'civilisation' with, the Satirist brands it with his usual pejoratives. Here is the same passage, only *with* the adjectives this time: '. . . when a chilly cave provided men with small homes, and a fire, a lars, and cattle and their masters enclosed in common shadow, when a mountain wife bestrewed her silvan bed with leaves, and straw, and hides of neighbouring wild beasts . . ., bearing paps for hefty babes to drink and often shaggier than her acorn-belching spouse' . . . *Some* of this material 'belongs' to the cliché—the nearness to nature, the breast-feeding . . . Some of it can be made to 'fit'—the 'smallness' of self-sufficiency, the 'make-do' mattresses . . . But just where does it start to become a self-satirising caricature for *you*? Is it with the 'neighbour beasts' and the '*mountain* wife'? (Is this J, the translator or you that finds a 'mountain wife' hard to take, then? As if a 'mountainous wife' to go with a 'Man-mountain'? Do you want women to be 'petite', *thin* things, then . . . ? Gotcha?) Or do you 'survive' till the 'paps' and 'acorns'? Has J hit on a truth here, that the routines of primitivism have always idealised as natural Cave-*Men*? Doesn't Tarzan swoop down on a Jane-whose-Make-up-must-show? How can a Woman be an ideal if she isn't attractive (*sc.* to men)? Answers . . . ?

  J 6 gathers together in a Sexth 'chapter' of *his* 'Themes in Roman Satire' all he wants to add about 'Women and Sex' to the panorama of Social Life in his first book (1–5): the flood of traditional 'fun' on the topic of woman-baiting. Is it easy to recognise that it's an old joke-fantasy when he puts women up as the active, aggressive and even violent ones, creatures of raw, animal sexuality? Is it harder to espy through the torrents of sarcasm unmistakably broad hints at the sentimentality which developed round the topic of marriage in imperial Rome: 'a cluster of relations characterised by affection, attachment, and reciprocity'[56]? See *this* 'new Man', his *simplicitas uxoria, deditus uni est animus*, 'a single and uxorious temperament, devoted to one'? (206–7. Sorry about the (self-satirical) pun in 'single'. Own up, though, you still can't fault a translation like 'uxorious'. *J* means this man is to sound just like a good *wife*.) Which are you going to fall for, Gentle Readers, I mean Suckers?

Here's just one such moment, in particularly glorious translation, where The Sisters are doing it for themSelves: shall I leave it to you to see if it's a *sentimental, sarcastic* and/or *sexy* moment? Here, anyway is some 'Women and Sex' to speak for itself: 'O inside their minds then what a heat of intercourse, their voice what lust saltating, what freshets of vintage liquor down their torrid legs! Saufeia, taking off her garland, challenges the pimps' slavegirls and wins a prize for floating hips. Herself adores the flow of haunching Medullina: the palm now rests with the ladies, virtue matches birth. Nothing during their play is simulated, all's done there for real, at which the son of Laomedon, now cold with age, and Nestor's hernia might inflame. Then the impatient itch, then simple womanhood and shouts repeated together from the entire grotto: "Now is it right. Admit the men." The adulterer dozes, to make haste and assume a hood a youth is charged; if he fails, there's an assault on slaves; remove the hope of slaves, comes even a hired water-carrier; if he's sought after and they want for humans, without delay will madam submit her bottom to be served by a donkey' (317–34. A religious occasion, this: that's why the women are congregated, for the Bona Dea's rites). In case you can't picture this scene through the translation, and I'm sure you wouldn't want to miss it, the idea is that the women need some men, slaves'd do or Ernie the milkman, or failing that at least a donkey . . . (The donkey, we could notice, is last but hardly 'least'.) And just so you don't miss this either, I should add that the 'climax' is going to be the scandal that a 'girl-psalterist' brought an enormous penis, 'a penis greater than Caesar's two *Anticatos*', into the grotto-shrine where the male gender was prohibited entry and even any *representation* 'of the other sex is . . . to be veiled' (337–41). This 'climax', does the penis come on its own or attached? Are the women not bothered which? Is that the point? Just how big, anyway, would a pair of Caesarian pamphlets make it? Is(n't) it all too obvious that this isn't going on 'inside *their* minds', at all, but instead every Man who assumes that size really matters, every Manjack 'son of Laomedon' (i.e. Priam), every Nestor? Let's call what's on show here '*MENtality*'. The scene *says* it is prurient, but shifts the prurience to catch women 'at it', the one scene where *men* are cast as 'the other sex' (the place where the male wears the veil), shifts the prurience away onto the senile ex-Men: But this doesn't work cleanly, since (don't you think?) Men *do* want to be kings, patriarchs, epic Fathers. In any case, if Men give up their throne because it's too 'chilly' for comfort, they give it up so that they can identify with the virile sex-machines the women are waiting for. (In fact they *aren't* waiting at all, they're sending-out for supplies of pronto penis. Actually, as usual, the fate of Priam and Nestor—awaiting all men—should remind you that there's a 'long-standing fallacy' here in the failure to specify, not 'penis', however huge, but 'Erection'. Perhaps we'd best not go into this?) If Men readers *would* like to be among 'the men' (*uiros*, 329), then they are caught in the shuttle of substitutions for 'men' that follow—'adulterer' 'youth' 'slaves' water-carrier' . . . 'donkey' . . . 'penis' . . . A slippery slope, this? Perhaps you won't be surprised to find that the next line after this scene begins 'And what *human* . . .' (*et quis . . . hominum*, 342). Does this rub in the way the would-be virile reader has been trapped into a worse-than-bestial self-projection onto his 'wedding-tackle'? *You*'d rather have or be an Erection than have or be a Human Being? Gotcha? Once more, we can see from putting together the way our translation reads to us—'freshets', 'torrid legs', 'girl-psalterist' and so on—how implicating this sex/text-uality is and is designed to be. Take that literally 'literary' yardstick (skip the sexual pun here, please), the comparison by which that 'penis' is sized up with a pair of literary texts . . . (by *Caesar*, notice . . .) and put it alongside the reminder that this location—and hence this literary *locus*, this 'set' for a set-piece, is supposed to veil maleness because it is itself essentially constituted as a place marked out for women as their own, it *is* what is veiled from 'the other sex'. The condition of male viewing of this grotty scene, as playmates, as literary figures from Homer, as readers of texts such as J 6, is that of the voyeur—with the added thrill of transgressive profanation of a traditional state-cult. When the women say 'Admit the men', the text has its bit of 'fun' with the *locus* and its in-mates: 'let them in', it means, 'let them (m) in, to get them (m) in to them (f), into them (f)'. To read this scene, then, is to 'penetrate' more veil than one; this is to see, yet not be seen, the very condition of reading. Satire is here pointing

up the role played in Literature by the reader's desire: *reflect on* any
irritations caused by the unfamiliarities of our translation: what is it that
you're *after*—'lucidity', perhaps, some language that you can 'see through',
through to what's 'happening' *inside* the grot, the women 'at it' . . . ? 'O
inside' *whose* 'minds'?

That scene was supposed to be (the Showman) showing us *femina
simplex*, 'simple womanhood'—'nothing . . . simulated, all . . . for real',
Woman as her equivalence with 'the impatient itch' (324-7). A little earlier,
we read of a Woman/Wife who is caught 'at it' and easily brushes her
husband aside by inventing Open Marriage and says 'What's sauce for the
Gander is sauce for the Goose: *homo sum*, 'I am *human*' (284). Put this
together with the Woman/Wife who a little earlier still wanted a slave's
guts for garters and asked her man what *she* meant to be a rhetorical
question but which I hope you may not be able to brush aside too easily,
ita seruus homo est?, 'So slaves are *human*?' (222). The question of what
being 'human' consists in, is to consist in, consists in for Romans and for
us, weaves its insistent way through this poem: pornotopia is just where
we are obliged to face our 'traditional opinions'. What *is* the place or
no-place, the utopia and dystopia, of Women in definitions of 'Humanity'?
Satire frames and so frames up humanist and atavist, civilised and
primitivesque, Theories, judgments and prejudices alike. No position is
authorised for the reader —no tenable position, that is. Each moment cries
out for Just-if-ication . . . (J's Muse always yells).

The overall conception of J 6 is what counts most, perhaps. This makes
Women come into being when they come into the reckoning for Men. They
are a topic because Men need Wives, those *objects* of exchange: *femina uoto
/ digna tuo . . . quod securus ames quodque . . . excerpere possis* (60-2), 'a
woman worthy of your vows . . . aught that you'd love unworried, that you
could single out' (*quod* means 'a *thing* which'. 'Vows' and 'single out' are,
I guess, not *meant* to pun so atrociously in this context, but enjoy the 'fun').
In this slice of 'Men's Talk', the idea is presented to us through the
addressee 'Postumus'. (I.e. one whose conception cost a Man his life: a
posthumous son is his own father from birth, the boy in the place of the
paterfamilias . . . His predicament distils those of all of Men? 'Mumma's
Boys' all.) The idea is that *no* women are worth marrying, as is plain before
a boy 'takes the plunge' and is discovered to the full when he's under their
thumb. (See how familiar all this is? 'Fun'?) Let's just suppose for a moment
the impossible: that there could be a reader who *does* get convinced by
every single one of J's 'examples' of No-good Women/Wives. That
reader—let's say 'that Postumus'—would join in a Graeco-Roman myth

with the figure of Hippolytus, beyond the pale of humanity, in 'the self's radical refusal of the Other'.[57] Maybe this age-old core of 'Maleness', the verbal 'freedom' to badmouth the World into existence, has no future. If it re-enforces a hierarchy of Man over Woman, the Self making itself complete by the rejection of its Other, all the same it can't acquiesce in its self-identification as the Erection. (As we've 'seen', donkeys have them, too, they're detachable and one day there'll be only penis and no more Erection for any men . . .) It aspires to a 'Humanity', some way of being civilised which aims 'higher' and 'deeper' than the crotch . . . But then where would 'la différence' between the sexes be? (Does sexuality differentiate minds and hearts?) If Satire shows you any of this *by* performing it, can its Showman also show you how thoroughly 'Maleness' has monopolised the past? Here you are invited to read 'against the grain', to become aware of, and to beware, the ways that 'traditional opinions' seek to naturalise themselves in nostalgia, in disavowal, in the cancellation of a history of 'human' being . . .

  (c) A final word, on J's most audacious performance, J 9.[58] Here J meets his match in dialogue shared with Naevolus (i.e. 'Mr. Mole', or—in case this gives the wrong impression—'Warty'). How shall I re-present it to you? 'It is an ugly, sordid subject and J presents it without moralising, and lets the stench of corruption speak for itself. This is indeed one of the most powerful of the satires'.[59] Does *this* introduction present it 'without moralising'? None of us, J, commentators, translators, readers, you nor I *can* let the material of Satire 'speak for itself'. That's just the point. Let's (try to) let it:

  (i) Poor thing, Naevolus looks worried, ill and thin. He's worked hard, as a 'client' should, for his patron(s). This 'family man', satisfied with his dear little—but not-*too*-little—homestead, has been shabbily rewarded. This after he's fathered children on a properly virgin wife—he's hoping to make it to the 3.0-children status that the Roman state rewards with tax-benefits—and through long devoted service, he's done so much to bring pleasure into his Lordship's life, to keep his marriage to her Ladyship off the rocks. All this good friend wants are some modest creature comforts, security for his dotage . . .

  (ii) Here's a 'Man' for you: since 'First impressions last longest' (says Prejudice . . .), we'll tell you how he looks. He *looks* like he's got what's coming to him, 'like vanquished Marsyas' (2). 'A satyr', then, i.e. the sex-crazy-bestial-Otherness-within-the-Male. *He* got his come-uppance from Apollo. The god of music and poetry . . . Punishment followed pride: he was, not torn off a strip, but 'flayed alive'. A promise from Satire, then, of defeat and victimisation? Simultaneously, he looks like one Ravola 'when caught out rubbing Rhodope's groin with his wet beard' (4). I'm not sure you can picture that? If 'Mr. Hoarse' (*Ravola*) was with 'Rosie' (*Rhodope*), 'clearly a prostitute', just how was he 'caught out'? (The word *deprensus* is 'normally' used of an adulterer.) Don't ask: your mind has enough to cope with in conjuring, in conjuring up, the superimposition 'Marsyas/Ravola'. From Greek myth to Latin 'reality', gods to whores, pain to farce, music to sex, the Satyr's blowing cheeks to the RoMan's dripping chin . . . (A red herring, too, and in retrospect 'fun', as the poem fastens deceptively on heterosex-minus-Erection for its first sexual characterisation of 'the pervert'. Is this an instance of the First Person being ruder than he seems by saying this *to* Naevolus or is he being more polite than he seems?) What this 'Man' does for his 'way of life' is (i) visit the temples, the places where women are 'bought' (ii) 'And what you don't tell, mounted their very husbands too' (20, 24–6. Is he a 'pervert' yet? Now? When, then?). Naevolus tells us his passport to a career has been 'the unique dimensions of' his 'member'—*for the mere sight draws men to a cinaedus*' (34, 37). He has, we could say (milking it for all it's worth), 'milked it for all it's worth'. But for what he's done for his 'patron', his 'wife would be still a maid. How often and by what means you begged this, you know well, and what was promised . . . Unstable unions, already splitting, and almost now dissolved, have in many homes been saved by adulterers . . . To you a little boy or girl was born of me . . . You accept them . . . these proofs of manhood (*argumenta viri*). You're now father' . . . you 'have parental rights . . . To these will be coupled many advantages besides if I bump the number up to three' . . . (72–90) Now Naevolus is ditched: Master 'procures himself another two-legg'd donkey' (92). 'J' is encouraging: 'Be not alarmed, you'll never lack a pathic friend while these hills stand secure' (130f.). But our 'Superstud' knows J's fine words are 'for the lucky ones. My Clotho and Lachesis' (Fates) 'are glad', *si pascitur inguine uenter*, 'if belly feeds on crotch' (135f.). In his own clear eyes, then, this Man literally 'lives on' his groin. Life, then, at subsistence level. Out in the *real* world.

(iii) The subject Naevolus—as you recall, 'an ugly, sordid subject and J presents it without moralising, and lets the stench of corruption speak for itself'—is 'a pervert who has been living as "husband" of an aristocrat pervert'.[60]

Does 'description' (iii) speak for itself? Does it (manage not to) moralise? Any more or any less than (i)? Or (ii)? ((iii) certainly fills in *lots* of 'gaps' so that it can read through the details to categorise the ménage as 'x living as "husband" of y'. A very 'recognisable' scene? Something our discourse knows to brand 'pervert' + 'pervert'? Two of a kind, then? Does J 9 see things this way?) *If* these three 'descriptions' of Naevolus re(-)present J 9 to you ('Wart' and all . . .), then *just* which is *your* version? Who *are* you? Do I know you? Would you want to know *me*? Like my essay, J 9 is presented as a dialogue. There is no privileged narrative presentation from 'J', only J's words to Naevolus and the replies. A selection of interacting 'fragments' of social discourse, a series of responses that interpret each other mutually and require you to fill the gaps between them—what is left unsaid, what is implied, what sorts of people are speaking, why we're 'eavesdropping' on them . . .—Even if J *did* give the 'authorised' version of 'Naevolus'—it's J's 'character', after all—you would know better than to give blanket acceptance to that Showman's 'point of view', you'd know (by now) that that's the best way to get egg on your face, to become the butt of the Satire? But this time, in any case, in *this* poem, there will be no 'escape' from its First Person's views of his victim. No escape indeed even *to* the First Person's 'views', since his words are supposed to be what he says out loud to Naevolus so they are mediated by all the decorums, conventionalities, strategies and power-plays which govern public utterances and social intercourse.

Yes, I chose that last word 'intercourse' advisedly: the politeness that I just described lubricates the civilised world of social exchange between human(e) beings. The question of the 'homosexual' nature of traditional society and its culture is opened up by our confrontation with the 'pervert', "husband", Naevolus: Can anyone who describes the man-to-man sex of J 9 as 'perverse' see why traditional opinions, theories and practices have patrolled their boundaries so carefully to stigmatise and repress women's participation in public conversation and thus to exclude all but the man-to-man versions of *that*? (Perhaps we could agree to call *these* 'per-versions' of 'intercourse'? They make Men each other's "husbands"?) 'Literature'—and as we saw, for example Philosophy, too—have precisely institutionalised the exclusion of Women as the rule of their operations. And this has been the force used to en-gender Culture, the force of phallogocentrism.

9 *Just like a woman?*

As I said at the start, Satire, like many other traditional practices and opinions, isn't *about* Women, it's about Men. About *Gender*. About whether you can find 'Justifications'. *Just, if* . . .

She said: It's hard. It's just hard. It's just kind of hard to say.
He said: Isn't it. Isn't it just. Isn't it just like a woman?

She said: It goes. That's the way it goes. It goes that way.
He said: Isn't it. Isn't it just like a woman?

She said: It takes. It takes one. It takes one to. It takesonetoknowone.
He said: Isn't it just like a woman?

She said. She said it. She said it to no. She said it to no one.
Isn't it. Isn't it just? Isn't it just like a woman?

L Anderson 1982, *It Tango*[61]

Notes

Notes to Introduction

1. An inscription (*CIL* 10.5382) found in the eighteenth century and lost in the nineteenth mentions a Juvenal who is identified by some with Juvenal the poet; see Highet 1954, 32-6. However, this identification is rather rash, not least because it relies on conjectural restoration of missing letters in the inscription. It is safer to conclude with Courtney 1980, 3-5 that the Juvenal named in the inscription is, at most, a relative of the poet.
2. For discussion of the *persona* theory see for example Anderson 1982, 3-10.

Notes to Mayer

1. Warde Fowler 1908, 269.
2. There is a sober account in Garnsey & Saller 1987, chapter 8 'Social relations'; perhaps inadequate weight is given even there to the dearth of evidence from the Republic.
3. A good illustration of the proper working of *officium* in difficult times is provided by C. Matius, a Roman knight, writing to Cicero about his continued loyalty to Julius Caesar after his assassination in *Ad fam.* 11.28.
4. Suetonius *Gramm.* 15.
5. Syme (1986) 383.
6. The word for client, *cliens*, is not in itself derogatory. Horace, for instance, styles one Vergilius (who is probably not the poet) 'the client of noble young men' at *Carm.* 4.12.15. If Vergilius was equestrian and the nobles were, as the word ought to mean, of senatorial rank, then *cliens* is correctly used, for it suggests an inferiority of rank: however rich they were, knights were not the social equals of senatorial families.
7. The story of Philippus and Mena, already referred to, may be a case in point. Philippus buys the helplessly urban Mena a farm as a joke, some amusement will flow from the incapacity of the auctioneer's agent to farm (*Epist.* 1.7.79). Philippus is like a cat with a mouse.
8. Gratwick 1982, 163.
9. For attacks on food, some of ambiguous tone, see Coffey 1976, 52.
10. The essay by Maguinness 1938, is humane and instructive; see also Kilpatrick 1986.
11. See Tacitus *Ann.* 1.54.3; Dio 54.17.4 refers to the dancer in 22 B.C., so his

arrival in Maecenas' company may have been a decade after Horace published his first book of satires. Nonetheless, Horace's concentration on men of literary taste in Maecenas' circle is suspiciously genteel.

12. That sympathy is given a fanciful astrological basis at *Carm.* 2.17.

13. Fraenkel 1957, 132 n.2, argues that this phrase attaches to the previous line and refers to the impartial praise Horace wants from his readers.

14. See also Cicero *De amic.* 66 and Seneca *De tranq. an.* 7.3 for *dulcis* of friendship.

15. Nisbet 1963, 61.

16. Butler 1909, 96.

17. See LaFleur 1979, Courtney 1980, 26–7.

18. So Sherwin-White 1966, 153 on *Ep.* 2.6.3.

19. The oddity of his account was noticed by Becker 1868, 230; see Braund & Cloud 1981, 197–8.

20. The practice of Pliny, set out by Sherwin-White 1966, 152 on *Ep.* 2.6.1, is instructive.

21. See Pliny *N.H.* 14.91.

22. The text with translation of the *Laus Pisonis* is in the Loeb volume entitled *Minor Latin poets*, edd. J.W. Duff & A.M. Duff (1935), 289–315.

23. At 1.101 'with us' he rhetorically associates himself with the indignities of the client, but nowhere else.

24. E.g. by Highet 1954, 132.

25. Courtney 1980, 491.

26. Courtney 1980, 152–3.

27. Garnsey & Saller 1987, 121–2.

28. This partiality was stressed by Nettleship 1895, 144; he attributed it to disappointments in the poet's own life. We have no evidence for this assumption.

29. It is worth noting that Pliny speaks of his 'friendship' with Martial in *Ep.* 3.21. Now at the time the poem was written Pliny was a senator and so the poet's social superior. Moreover there is only one poem by Martial on Pliny—the 'friendship' was not dearly bought.

30. At the time this poem was written Stella had probably not yet held office, but he was undoubtedly far superior to Martial socially and marked for high office already. But the use of *meus* points to intimacy, a breaking down of social barriers.

31. See especially White 1978.

32. Courtney 1980, 591–2.

Notes to Braund

1. Criticism of city life e.g. Seneca *Controv.* 2.1.11–12; 5.5. Praise of rustic ancestors e.g. *Controv.* 1.6.4, 2.1.8, also cf. Valerius Maximus 4.4.11, another

author closely reproducing the arguments and material of the rhetorical schools. The two themes are brought together in the criticisms of the rich for attempting to re-create the country in the city, in the form of waters and groves—'false groves' (*mentita nemora*)—within city houses (5.5).

2. Hodgart 1969, 129; cf. 135–7.
3. Kernan 1959, 7–8.
4. I draw a distinction between Juvenal the author and the voice we hear speaking in the poems. Satirists regularly use a mask, or *persona*, to present their satires, which should not be identified with the poet but viewed as a dramatic creation of the poet: see my Introduction to this volume. In potential cases of confusion, I will call the voice 'Juvenal' rather than Juvenal, as a reminder that the voice we hear is one created by the poet.
5. For a more detailed account of the structure of Satire 2, see Braund & Cloud 1981, 203–8.
6. Carcopino 1962, 304.
7. Paoli 1963, 37–40.
8. Walford 1875, 132–49. Green 1960, 175 comments that 'one of the main advantages Roman satire offers us is a picture of contemporary life—the details that conventional literature felt itself above mentioning. Open any standard work on Roman private antiquities—Friedländer, Marquardt, Carcopino—and you will find that Martial, Horace, and Juvenal are cited more often than all other literary sources added together.'
9. *caligatus* means 'wearing heavy boots', such as a muleteer (cf. Petronius *Satyr.* 69.5) or a soldier (cf. Juv. 16.24) might wear, and so implies a simple country-dweller who is accustomed to walking long distances.
10. For the ironic reversal of the *locus amoenus* at the start of Satire 3 see Williams 1984, 125. Imitation of country scenes in the city was a standard item in the rhetorical schools: see Seneca *Controv.* in note 1 above.
11. On the distinction between 'Juvenal' and Juvenal, see note 4 above.
12. The soothsayer who foretold the emperor Galba's death was called Umbricius: Pliny *N.H.* 10.19, Plutarch *Galba* 24, Tacitus *Hist.* 1.27; see *RE* 17 594–6, *RE* Suppl. 9A 1827: on inscriptions the name occurs in Etruria, Pompeii and Puteoli.
13. Rudd 1966, 143–6, with some caveats. On Cupiennius cf. Henderson in this volume, p.105.
14. Walsh 1970, 81 and 82. Modern examples are provided most obviously by Charles Dickens but also in works such as Gogol's *The Government Inspector*, see Highet 1962, 274 n. 50.
15. For Umbricius as *umbra*, shade, fleeing Rome, see Motto & Clark 1965, 275–6.
16. For Umbricius as parody of the departing virgin goddess Motto & Clark 1965, 271–5.
17. Fruelund Jensen (1986) independently proposes a very similar view of Umbricius' character. This is by no means the only place in Roman Satire where a character exposes his personality in his own words. Horace provides

several clear examples in his second Book of Satires, where for example Catius (*Sat.* 2.4) delivers a long speech on food which reveals that he takes the art of gastronomy far too seriously in elevating it to the level of philosophy—and makes himself ridiculous in the process (see Hudson in this volume, pp.80-1). Other characters who make themselves ridiculous through their own words in Horace Book 2 include Damasippus (2.3) and Davus (2.7). The same technique is used in Juvenal 1, where 'Juvenal' reveals his anger and extremism, which makes it difficult to take him entirely seriously (see Anderson 1982, 297–314). Perhaps the classic example of someone who exposes himself to ridicule by his words and conduct is Trimalchio in Petronius' *Satyrica*: Trimalchio continually reveals his lack of culture and breeding and taste in his pronouncements at the dinner-party.

18. Anderson e.g. 1982, 278.
19. For example, Ennius 112W; Sallust *BJ* 31.11: 'Will you, citizens of Rome, born in authority, endure slavery with patience?' Seneca specifically states that an emotive appeal to the 'citizens of Rome' was not the starting-point of a public speech but rather a climax: *Ep.* 15.7: 'No speaker cries "Help me, citizens of Rome" at the outset of his speech.' In Apuleius an old man appeals to the people with the formula *per fidem uestram, Quirites, per pietatem publicam* (*Met.* 2.27); and later occurs the humorous incident in which Lucius the ass tries to exclaim *porro Quirites* but can only utter *O* (*Met.* 8.29).
20. Carcopino 1962, 43 and 44–5.
21. Exactly the same point provides the witty climax to one of Martial's epigrams (3.52). Though Martial was not writing in the genre of satire, he undoubtedly shares Juvenal's satirical view of the world.
22. A garret, *tenebras* 225, literally 'darkness' and therefore 'squalid buildings' seems an appropriate place for a man called *Umbr*icius to live!
23. Carcopino 1962, 56.
24. E.g. the rich man's litter is described as if it were a war-ship, a 'huge Liburnian' galley (240); the image of the 'wave' (*unda*, 244) of pedestrians is one used of soldiers in epic (e.g. Silius Italicus 4.159); *obstat* (243) and *magno ... agmine* (244) are words appropriate in military contexts (for *obstat* cf. Statius *Theb.* 8.350; Lucan 7.152-3); the verb *ferit*, 'strikes', repeated in anaphora (245), is another word found in elevated epic descriptions of battles but with weapons rather different from the 'elbow' (*cubito*) and 'hard pole' (*assere duro*) (*ferit* in Virgil occurs in military contexts with a variety of weapons: *hasta Aen.* 10.346, *saxo* 10.415, *telo ... trabali* 12.295, *ense* 12.304, 458; cf. in particular Turnus who *hunc uenientem cuspide longa, | hunc mucrone ferit* 12.510-11; cf. also Lucan 3.666 *ferit ense*); and so on.
25. The change from *portitor* to the Greek word *porthmeus* is perhaps explained by the fact that Charon is a character from Greek mythology but also by the scornful tone with which Juvenal invests Greek words.
26. Lucretius achieves a similar satirical effect when he cites conventional sentiments of people mourning for a loved one—only to criticise them for their

folly (3.894–911). From this passage, lines 894–9 are often quoted out of context, without attention to the ironic spirit here and to the parodic and satirical touches in the surrounding context (e.g. 904–8): for discussion see Kenney 1971, *ad loc.*

27. E.g. death caused by a falling chamber-pot, Ehrenberg & Jones 1976, no. 312; Paoli who takes this section literally (1963, 39) would be better advised to turn to these other sources.

28. This is a likely interpretation of a problematic text.

29. Paoli 1963, 38 fails to see the exaggeration here.

30. This scene is reminiscent of the similarly unequal beating-up of Sosia by Mercury in Plautus *Amph.* 292–462, e.g.: MERC. Any man who comes this way will eat fists. SOS. Oh no! I don't want to eat at this time of night. It wasn't long ago I dined . . . and MERC. Speak up, what are you doing here? SOS. To give you someone to punch, and especially 379 *quia uaniloquo's, uapulabis.*

31. *obstet* 71 cf. Juv. 3.243 *obstat,* also Hor. *Sat.* 2.6.30 *obstat; tignum* 73 cf. Juv. 3.246 *tignum; lutulenta* 75 cf. Juv. 3.247 *luto.*

32. Lactantius *Div. Instit.* 5.9.20.

33. E.g. Lucilius criticises a Syrian (652–3W), a Syrophoenician (540–1W), Lydian clothing (12W) and a Hellenomaniac (87–93W).

34. Syme 1958, 776–7.

35. Townend 1973 provides examples of the 'literary substrata' to Satires 4 and 7 in particular.

36. He calls it his *arcem,* 'stronghold'. The word usually denotes the citadel or fortified high point in a city, in particular in Rome; so his use of it here in the phrase *in arcem ex urbe remoui,* 'I've left town for my castle', is surprising and almost paradoxical and challenges us to realise the *symbolic* value of the word.

37. This seems to be the point of the Aesop fable (314), which ends with the country mouse saying 'I prefer to live frugally but in freedom and security'. Observe that his home in the country, 'on a cliff edge in the woods', line 91, is perhaps to be seen as a mouse equivalent of Horace's *arx,* 'castle'.

38. Wall-paintings from Rome and Pompeii reflect a 'soft primitive' view of the countryside with their portrayals of herdsmen and pastoral scenes. For a discussion and illustrations of pastoral scenes on wall-painting, see Leach 1974, 83–95, who uses Vitruvius 7.5.2 as her starting-point.

39. The country mouse is the inverse of Virgil's Tityrus who in *Eclogues* 1 goes to the city and becomes dependent to ensure his survival in the country; the country mouse's visit to the city here endangers his life.

40. E.g. the praise of country life which ends Book 2 of the *Georgics,* lines 458–542.

41. E.g. Seneca *Ep.* 87.41, Livy pr. 11–12. For the proper conduct of those from country towns see Tacitus *Ann.* 3.55, Pliny *Ep.* 1.14.6.

42. Lines 90–7: the philosophical flavour of these lines is well explained by West 1974, 74–5: the city mouse is a pseudo-Epicurean whose message, 'enjoy the good things of life', is so pretentiously presented as to be an amusing parody.

43. Thus Kilpatrick 1986, 71.
44. Cf. Kilpatrick 1986, 91.
45. This is an interesting combination of Horatian material on city and country: it is Horace's *city* mouse who expresses the same hedonist or pseudo-Epicurean view.
46. Cf. again *BJ* 41.2–5, also Velleius 2.1.1.
47. So Highet 1954, e.g. 17, Gérard 1976, 10.
48. See Balsdon 1969, 196–9 on suburban villas of the rich.
49. In the case of Pliny *Ep.* 1.24 we may even have a case of the literary tradition influencing life. Here to the writer Suetonius seeking a suitable country estate, Pliny suggests, rather playfully, that 'scholars turned landowners . . . need no more land than will suffice to clear their heads and refresh their eyes as they stroll around their grounds and tread their single path, getting to know each one of their precious vines (*uiteculas*) and counting every little fruit tree (*arbusculas*)' (*Ep.* 1.24.4).
50. Manius Curius Dentatus, who was leader in the wars against the Samnites and conquered Pyrrhus, was a type of old Roman frugality. Seneca *Ad Helv.* 10.8 tells the story of how envoys of the Samnites found him cooking vegetables.
51. Juvenal's debt to Horace here is clear, with 'warm cafe', *calidae . . . popinae*, recalling *Epist.* 1.14.21 'greasy cafe', *uncta popina*.
52. For the same combination of ideas cf. 14.161: in the good old days people were content with a modest plot and self-sufficiency as opposed to *avaritia*.
53. Thanks to colleagues at Exeter University who have heard versions of this chapter (in city and country settings!) for their valuable comments; they are not to be held responsible for what I have made of them.

Notes to Cloud

I am obliged to Professor J.A. Crook for many helpful suggestions; he is not responsible for what I have made of them. I would also like to express my gratitude to the Research Board of Leicester University for paying for visits to libraries in Cambridge and London to consult material not available in Leicester.

1. There are other difficulties in detecting original material. As happens nowadays with editions of legal works, the works of the great jurists were regularly re-edited and updated after their deaths. Naturally enough, Tribonian, Justinian's director of the Digest project, and his assistants used updated editions for their excerpts. Consequently, the excerpts from the jurists of the second and third centuries that we read in the Digest could, at least theoretically, be

very different texts from those actually composed by the jurists. Johnston 1989 on interpolation in the legal sources.

2. Twelve Tables 5.4 (= Bruns 1909, 23 and Girard & Senn 1977, 35). Although the phrase *proximus heres* is used occasionally in the Digest, it has a different and non-technical meaning.

3. Persius has taken the name of Nerius from Hor. *Sat.* 2.3.69 where Nerius would appear to be a foolhardy banker who will back a loan to the bankrupt Damasippus. In that situation it is Damasippus, not Nerius, who has on his side the god of luck (there Mercury, not Hercules). The farmer finding buried treasure by grace of Hercules derives from Hor. *Sat.* 2.6.10–12; Persius has changed Horace's urn into a preserving jar (*seria*). Presumably his motive is partly sheer love of variation, partly to emphasise the preposterousness of the prayer—people are even less likely to bury treasure in a preserving jar than in an urn!—and partly for the pun on *serius* (= serious)—the prayer is serious enough for the petitioner, but frivolous to the Stoic speaker. I have referred in the text to the play on Hor. *Sat.* 2.5.45–50.

4. For Persius' use of disease imagery, cf. Dessen 1968, 43–4 n.13, 47–8 and Bramble 1974, 35–8.

5. See Tacitus *Ann.* 11.6–7 and Crook 1967, 90–1.

6. In 60 B.C. a grateful client, L. Papirius Paetus, made Cicero a present of a library of Greek and Latin books (*Ad Att.* 1.20.7); Hortensius had received from Verres a costly statue of the sphinx as a reward for undertaking his defence in 70 B.C. But their younger contemporaries, P. Clodius and C. Curio, took fat fees in defiance of the law (Tacitus *Ann.* 11.7).

7. Unfortunately, there is no alternative at times to leaving *iudex* untranslated, for the word can mean either 'juryman' or the single 'judge' to whose decision the urban praetor in most cases would hand over a dispute in civil law between the two parties. Neither kind of *iudex* was a professional and this fact makes the word 'judge' a most misleading word as a translation of *iudex* in the second sense. (See Crook 1967, 78–83 for the way in which the single *iudex* worked.) *Pace* Jenkinson 1980, 47, the speaker is probably envisaging Marcus Dama as a *iudex* of the second kind, since 'You quail with Jones on the bench?' (Rudd's translation) makes more sense if the recently emancipated slave was the sole adjudicator and in any case Jones/Dama would not have got on to the panel of jurors without having equestrian status. Perhaps surprisingly, a humble citizen could adjudicate between two parties, provided that he was chosen jointly by both of them.

8. The Latin words are *uertigo* and *turbo*.

9. The turning presumably symbolises the slave's turning away from his master, from the dependence of slavery to the independence of citizenship. In fact, even at the institutional level the symbolism is suspect: quite apart from other general disabilities incurred by the new citizen or freedman (*libertus*), he was obliged to perform a number of services for his former master. (See Crook 1967, 50–5.)

10. Suetonius *Dom.* 8.3.
11. Marongiu 1977. For an authoritative account of *fideicommissa* see now Johnston 1988, esp. 42–75 on secret trusts.
12. There were no censuses and therefore no *classici*; it is hard to see how the *lex Voconia* would work. For other arguments, see Dixon 1985 and Dixon 1988, 89–90. For the motivation behind the very patriarchal-looking provisions of the Voconian Law, see Gardner 1986, 170–8.
13. Ulp. *Reg.* 16.3, sometimes thought to justify a distinction between husband and wife, in this regard seems to me, no more than to Buckland & Stein 1963, 293.3, to do nothing of the sort.
14. Lucilius 251W, Hor. *Sat.* 2.5.75–84; Ovid *Am.* 2.19.57–60; Apuleius *Apol.* 75.
15. It was attacked first of all by Daube 1965 and then by Watson 1971, 175–6 and as vigorously rebutted by Crook 1973.
16. Plautus *Curculio* 622, *intestatus uiuito* (likewise *id. Miles Gloriosus* 1417) implies a curse *intestatus moriatur*, 'May he die intestate', for the joke to work. And some of the evidence cited by Daube 1965 and Watson 1971, 175–6 seems to me to boomerang: for example, that Horace made a will on his death-bed (at the end of *Vita Horati*) suggests that he did care about intestacy rather than that he did not.
17. Just as *'heredes* uetat esse *suos'* (he disinherits his own flesh and blood) at 10.237 must suggest the legal phrase *sui heredes*—who were those who inherited automatically if there was no will, i.e. essentially a man's sons and daughters.
18. For example, Aemilius' equestrian statue of himself (7.127–8) shows him one-eyed—presumably the other had dropped out—and his spear is bent, no doubt like Aemilius himself, because made of inferior metal. There is something gimcrack about even the successful lawyer!
19. See Grellet-Dumazeau 1858, 113–30. For reasons for in general trusting Martial rather than Juvenal, see Cloud 1989. However, in this case Martial is supported by the Younger Pliny.
20. See Cloud 1989 for other examples.
21. Cf. Horace *Sat.* 2.3.143; Persius *Sat.* 5.147; Martial 1.103.9, 2.53.4, 2.49.
22. Centurions they would have to have been. Centurions are mentioned at line 17 and no lower rank would have had sufficient status to be in any way comparable to the *iudices* assigned by the praetor to hear normal actions. Not the least of the differences between the world of satire and the real world of Hadrianic Rome lies in the emblematic function of the centurion in the satirists—the malodorous and Philistine bully—and the status enjoyed by the centurion in real life; for the purposes of the law he ranked as a member of the superior class (*honestiores*) like a senator or knight and thus escaped the drastic penalties visited upon the lower orders (*humiliores*), such as working the mines for non-capital offences and crucifixion or being thrown to the lions for capital offences. He enjoyed the status that indisputably qualified him for acting as a judge in a dispute between two soldiers (cf. Cavenaile 1958, no. 212, to be dated to the principate of Claudius or Nero). Durry's theory 1935, 95, that

Juvenal is really talking about retired members of the praetorian and urban cohorts (*euocati*) but speaks of centurions because the Latin word *euocatus* will not scan in dactylic hexameters, is completely superfluous.

23. Reading *adsit*, Collins's attractive emendation, but the reading of most manuscripts, *absit* (= 'would be away'), though less pointed, will make sense.

24. Pylades, Orestes' faithful friend, who helps him to take vengeance on his mother Clytemnestra, and her lover Aegisthus, for their murder of his father Agamemnon, is the archetypal loyal comrade, as in Ovid (*Rem. Am.* 589).

25. In *Sat.* 5.153 and 8.43 Juvenal refers to the Servian Wall as the Rampart (*agger*) as does Horace (*Sat.* 1.8.15). But the word *agger* could as naturally refer to the rampart of a military camp and when Juvenal writes: 'who would support you [*or* absent himself: see n.23] so far from the city, who would be such a pal as to come *molem aggeris ultra*', he could mean 'beyond (i.e. inside) the massive rampart (of the camp)'. Knowing the artfulness of Juvenal, even in old age, I would suggest that he means, all along, to suggest both ideas, for the reason suggested in the text.

26. See reference in n.22.

27. There is another example of fudging in the passage. It is not clear whether or not 'the mighty calves against large benches' of line 14 belong to 'the whole cohort' of line 20 which is against the civilian party. Is this a case of the judge having a posse of soldier advisors—rather surprising in a case of assault—who if the centurion finds for the plaintiff can be relied upon to rough him more thoroughly than ever defendant did in the case being tried or are the mighty calves those of the centurion himself and the large benches a poetic plural?

28. Kelly 1966, 120–31.

29. It is often said that Labeo and Alfenus cannot be the famous jurists who bore those names because Labeo was too young and Alfenus Varus too distinguished—he had been consul in 39—to be taxed with humble origins by the son of an ex-slave, such as Horace was. Nevertheless, the conjunction of precisely those two names is too remarkable to be a mere coincidence. And Labeo was notorious for his lack of prudence and restraint (cf. Gellius 13.12.2; Suetonius *Aug.* 54).

30. 104–6; the presence of adulterers here is a typical piece of Horatian foolery; there was no *law* against adultery until Augustus introduced one in 18 B.C. However, the perils of adultery had been graphically described in the previous satire and adulterers—as well as thieves and murderers—are mentioned at the beginning of the next satire (1.4.3–4) as topics suitable for Aristophanic comedy and satire alike. The satirist, typically, has put literary needs before fidelity to social fact.

31. The passage discussed in the previous note goes on to state that female private parts (Horace uses a vulgar word, *cunnus*, not to be found in the other satirists) have been a particularly vile cause of war before Helen. Quite apart from the coarseness of the reference to Helen, the notion that wars could be caused by feminine charms was regarded as absurd even in the fifth century

B.C., as Euripides' treatment of the topic in the *Helen* shows.

32. *'Quartae sit partis Vlixes,' audieris, 'heres'.* (100–1) = 'You have heard the words: "a fourth part of my estate is to go to Ulysses".'

33. Wolf 1985. For an earlier study of Satire 1.9 and Roman Law see Paratore 1964.

34. The passage must refer to the appearance of the plaintiff and defendant before the praetor for two reasons: the phrase *rapit in ius* is only used of the first stage of a lawsuit, known as the *in iure* stage, and the ear-tweaking ritual whereby a person signifies to the plaintiff that he is prepared to act as witness to the arrest takes place only as a preliminary to the first stage.

35. . . . *et casu tunc respondere uadato | debebat, quod ni fecisset perdere litem* (36–7). A stickler for syntax could argue that as *fecisset* is in the subjunctive, it merely represents what was in the pest's mind (virtual *oratio obliqua*) and not Horace's view of the law: the pest may think in terms of losing his case, but Horace may know better.

36. See Leeman 1983, and, more briefly, 1982.

37. Trebatius is made to say: 'if a party shall have composed bad poems / evil songs (*mala . . . carmina*) against another, there is law and a trial.' The 'evil songs' of the fifth century B.C. were certainly rhythmical spells, as the context of the law shows.

38. Horace uses the same section of the Twelve Tables in *Epist.* 2.1.152–3. See Brink's edition (1982) *ad loc.*

39. For example, Smith 1951 esp. 177–8.

Notes to Hudson

1. Translation of the German proverb 'Der mensch ist was er isst'.

2. Seneca *Ad Helv.* 10.8–9.

3. Pliny *N.H.* 9.172.

4. Livy 39.6, Pliny *N.H.* 10.140. Professional cooks are supposed to have arrived after the war with Antiochus. Such attitudes to foreign foods are not exclusive to antiquity. From more recent times, see for example the extract from Joseph Addison writing in *The Tatler* no. 148 (21st March 1709) of a sirloin relegated to a side-table, cited by Mennell 1985, 126: 'I . . . could not see, without some indignation, that substantial *English* dish banished in so ignominious a manner, to make way for *French* kickshaws.'

5. Boar, peacock, mullet (and turbot) appear with some regularity in the satires and are consistently noted for being, respectively, symbolic of hospitality, valuable for their appearance and notoriously expensive when large.

6. The voice we hear in the satires, not the real Horace, Persius or Juvenal. For discussion see the Introduction to this volume.

7. Hippocrates devoted whole books to the subject, including his 'On the healthy

regime', prescribing what the ordinary man should eat to maintain health, and three books on the factors of health, exercise and diet.

8. Two of the most famous moral maxims of the ancient world, inscribed on the temple of Apollo at Delphi and attributed to the seven sages. Ofellus in Hor. *Sat*. 2.2.53–5 advises steering the middle course between excesses of gluttony and frugality. Juvenal in *Sat*. 11.27–38 impresses on us the importance of knowing oneself, or rather the limits of one's spending power.

9. Hor. *Sat*. 2.2. and 6; Pers. 6; Juv. 11.

10. For the enormous range of farm produce see Cato *De Agricultura* 6–8, 160; Varro *De Re Rustica* 1.2.6–7, 58–9, 2.11.3, 2.9.17–15.2; Columella *De Re Rustica* 10, 11.3.14–18; Celsus 2.18–33.

11. Hor. *Sat*. 2.2.118–25 (including 'Pythagorean' beans, Gellius 4.11.); Pers. 6. 67–9 (nettles and smoked pig's cheek, a purposely unattractive version); Juv. 11.64–76.

12. Athenaeus *Deipnosophistae* 274. The same combination is given religious overtones in Ovid *Fast*. 6.169–82 (and contrasted with luxury foods such as peacock and fish) and *Met*. 8.648–79 (where Baucis and Philemon entertain the Gods).

13. See Frayn 1979, 39. The 'Moretum' in the Appendix Virgiliana seems to describe a recipe for a sort of herb cheese.

14. On the derivation of 'Ofellus', cf. Chapter 2 n. 13 above.

15. Hor. *Sat*. 1.3.13–15. A table, salt and a coat are all that the inconsistent Tigellius requires.

16. Hor. *Sat*. 1.10.3 (perhaps a hint that we are to take Ofellus' 'wisdom' with a pinch of salt!). According to Pliny *N.H.* 31.89, Varro described the early Romans eating salt with bread as a dish in itself. Salt was transported to Rome from the salt beds at the mouth of the Tiber and thence along the 'Via Salaria' (salt road) to central Italy (André 1981, 193).

17. West 1974, 71.

18. If anything this is 'hard primitivism', that is, a version of country life that acknowledges, but still idealises frugality.

19. On which see Colton 1964.

20. See n.10 above.

21. For example at Pompeii Reg. 1;1.8 the variety of pastries enjoyed in Pompeii is denoted by the use of special names for cooks depending on the type of pastry they cooked: *placentarii, crustularii, dulciarii, clibanarii, labarii*.

22. Lines 193–202; the occasion is the holiday for the Megalesian Games. Weisinger 1972 also discusses the theme of escape, but does not develop the idea of the 'country style' meal in the city. The satirist's maxim 'know thyself' is explored in Felton & Lee 1972.

23. Martial 2.43.9–10, discussed by Colton 1964, 42.

24. E.g. Statius *Silv*. 4.4.61; Tacitus *Ann*. 2.61.

25. There is, of course, no such thing as an Arabian elephant. Courtney 1980 on 11.126 suggests that 'Petra was on the trade-route from India so it was regarded

as the source of the ivory which it only transmitted'. But what if Juvenal was aware of this discrepancy and was, therefore, incorporating Arabia completely on account of its newness and strangeness?

26. Rudd 1966, 206; Classen 1978 argues that Catius' lecture has a rather loose structure which contributes to Horace's characterisation of him.

27. Hor. *Sat.* 1.3.7 encompasses the meal with the formula *ab ovo usque ad mala* (from eggs to apples).

28. Aristotle *Hist. Anim.* 6.2.2 in which he discusses the relative qualities of male and female eggs.

29. Ennius *Hedyphagetica* (a kind of Cooks' tour of the world) has already parodied the gastronomic catalogue type of literature as exemplified in the 'Peri Edesmaton' of Archestratos (Athenaeus *Deipnosophistae* 163).

30. Size (39–40); appearance (23–7); place of origin (31–3).

31. Boar has a similar consistency of treatment in Horace's satire: 2.2.42, 3.73, 4.41, 8.6.

32. Although it is not always easy to judge the function of a room from archaeological remains there are many examples in the houses of the Bay of Naples area, which though not necessarily typical of *Rome* nevertheless illustrate the importance accorded to dining-rooms by some Romans: for example, at Pompeii in the House of the Lovers, and at Herculaneum where the house of the Mosaic Atrium had a dining room built to maximise an uninterrupted sea view. At the uppermost end of the social scale the dining rooms at Hadrian's villa at Tivoli were designed to benefit most from the view of the gardens.

33. Vitruvius 6.4.2.

34. Elaborate wall-paintings and mosaics are found in the *triclinia* of the humblest homes, and seem to overstep the status of the house as suggested by other rooms, e.g. at Herculaneum where the House of the Neptune and Amphitrite mosaic, a small house, has a brilliant mosaic overlooked from the *triclinium.*

35. Hence the pointedly humble accompaniments to Horace's solo meal. Seneca and Petronius get maximum moral value from extravagant descriptions of dining room decoration and furniture, e.g. Seneca *Ep.* 110.12 (gilded couches and jewelled furniture); Petronius *Satyr.* 30–4, 67–8.

36. As an idealised philosophical forum at which the greatest thinkers are present. For discussion of the symposium in its historical context see Murray 1983.

37. Hor. *Sat.* 2.8.16, 43; 73.

38. Juv. 5.14, 130, 137, 161; 71, 81; 115.

39. Juv. 5.170; 157–8.

40. Apicius 8.1: ten recipes for boar. Flower & Rosenbaum 1958, 181–3.

41. Homer *Il.* 9.529–99; Ovid *Met.* 8.270–444 in which the boar is the 'servant and avenger of Diana' (272).

42. Martial 7.27.1–2, 9.49, 13.93, cf. 13.41.2.

43. Martial 2.43, 3.49, 60, 68, 85, 6.11, 9.2, 48; Pliny *Ep.* 2.6. All dealing with the unfair treatment of clients at table.

44. Another ironic allusion to Martial, 2.10.5. Claudius is supposed to have died of mushroom poisoning. Perhaps this is a hint that those who wield power are prey to special kinds of risks.
45. Morford 1977, 245 tabulates the comparative menus.
46. Cf. Plat. *Phaed.* 83d.
47. This is not to say that the ancient sources had no opinion on the relationship of eating and bathing. Galen 7.702–3 warns against bathing immediately after eating. This is still no reason to imagine that death in the bath was as common as the satirists like to imply.

Notes to Henderson

1. A harder, more or less 'literary', version of this essay will (have) appear(ed) as Henderson 1989. Relations between the papers are reciprocal, even deconstructive. (No '???' in the other one, no '!!!' in this . . .)
2. I am alluding here to the justly famous parable of Borges 1970, 62–71, *Pierre Menard, author of Don Quixote*. I very much hope you will make a point of reading this.
3. Kennedy 1984 sharply pierces through the general 'complicity' of critics with Horace: you'ld get a lot out of this little essay. He addresses one of the key questions for all Latinists: what stake do you have in agreement with H(orace)? Reading *H*, and especially reading H's *Satires*, revolve(s) round this issue, I think.
4. The invaluable repertory Lefkowitz & Fant 1982 restricts itself to one lemma from Roman Satire. It repays some thought—don't just *use* it—: their item 157 translates 'excerpts' from Juvenal 6 under the (strange-to-provocative) heading 'Juvenal on women in general'; it appears as the final entry in a chapter on 'Rome' called 'Wives, Mothers, Daughters'. The 'Greece' section of the book has 'Wives, Daughters, Friends' for its matching chapter heading (the only exception to the otherwise complete match of identical headings between the two cultures' chapters). The questions thrust themselves upon us: what sense *is* there in opposing 'Greece'—'Greece'?—to 'Rome'? (A high proportion of the 'sources' come from imperial Roman Greeks: how *have* Roman Fant and Graeco-Christian Lefkowitz negotiated their boundaries?) And, more intriguingly, did 'Greeks' have somehow less 'Mothers' as 'Romans' had less 'Friends'? Do you see how 'Sourcebook' is (supposed to be) a self-justifying rubric? So frustrating for us to be given our aids for study but denied the logic, Theory or prejudice they embody, isn't it? Epigrams aside, just one other piece of Latin poetry is included (H, *Epode* 5): the editors right-mindedly (I expect) decided to 'omit . . . from the book . . . literary texts readily available in paperback that should be read in their entirety' but reproduced 'familiar texts, like . . . selections from J(uvenal)'s sixth satire . . . for the reader's convenience'

(Preface xv f. At once we're intrigued once more: did they 'try' to keep J out? Did they feel daft offering a book without J 6 in it and calling it 'Women's Life in Greece & Rome'? Did they 'shake their heads' and accept that unfortunately courses on Roman Women were going to carry on featuring this (in)famous text, whatever *their* views on the matter? Is it a reluctance that puts it at the end of its chapter: J 6's excerpts are given their set of informative scholarly footnotes, but no line references or markers of omissions; they are not contextualised at all in their poem (there is no hint of how huge a poem it is—by the way, it's *huge*—, I guess it's (going to have to be) 'familiar' already: yet there is room to preface it with a note that may clear J of 'hating women' . . .). How was the order and economy of items decided and what are we to conclude from them? This business of organising and labelling categories is so determinative, so 'theory-laden' in and through all its pragmatisms. Isn't it? 'Whenever possible we have tried to let the documents speak for themselves' . . . (Preface xvi. They do add cautionary notes here: *don't* skip them.)

5. Balsdon 1962 is a book length study of 'Roman Women' which is perhaps more a feat of organisation than of analysis: if you read his little Preface you will find a charmingly 'literary' text of layered disclaimers. Could you imagine *anyone* today, less than 30-odd years later, writing this way: 'The book is written in the belief that the subject is interesting . . . I have been trying for thirty years to write a book on the late Roman Republic . . . A few years ago I tried a new attack on the period; I tried to approach it through its women . . . The result was a paper . . . which I read to so many branches of the Classical Association that the reading of it became not merely a habit but a disease.' (Just like a woman . . .) 'Cauterization was the only cure; it had to be published . . . After that, Mr Colin Haycraft of The Bodley Head bullied me' (as 'husband' wife?) 'into taking these women' (sic) 'and turning them into a book' (9f.)? Why not? What's changed? Plenty of J in *this* book . . .

6. Steiner 1982, 115. A memorable definition, this. *She* may have meant 'limitless' to straddle undeterminably between 'so vast as to include everywhere' and 'defying all attempts to bound, define, master it'. *I* certainly do.

7. Rudd 1986—expert and reliable, the work which, I know, you will certainly be relying on in your studies of Roman Satire, so I want to write this extended nasty note to help you raise critical questions about it right away—: Chapters, '1 Aims and Methods, 2 Freedom and Authority, 3 Style and Public, 4 Class and Patronage, 5 Greek and the Greeks, 6 Women and Sex'. For a tantalising glimpse of explanation for this strategy, *don't* skip the Preface (ix-xii. I half think *you*'re supposed to): 'A little thought will show that the six themes I have chosen overlap. So it was necessary to make certain decisions of a somewhat arbitrary kind . . . The opinions behind this book are traditional. I mention five . . . Those five opinions . . . are accepted as truisms within the humanist tradition. Outside it they are widely contested'. This is again all so frustrating for us readers: does R(udd), or does R not, realise that 'themes' are the things you choose as your organisational units *if* you want to slice up your

material into artificially separate chunks (and then apologise for doing so)? This is just the sort of self-justifying work that the term 'theme' performs, isn't it? Perhaps he is *reminding* us of this, perhaps all too gently? How is it possible for R to remark on some of the arbitrarinesses involved in all five of his Chapters 1–5 and not mention just chapter 6, 'Women and Sex'? He says: 'Neoteric or neo-Callimachean material, which appears under the heading 'Greek and the Greeks' . . . could, indeed, have gone elsewhere, but it seemed to provide the best balance when placed in Chapter Five'. Is 'the best balance' achieved for Chapter Six, then, by putting it last as a matter of 'last but not least', a supplementariness, an after-thought, a replica of J's postponement of 'Women' to his Satire 6, in a separate book of its own, after the mannish Satires 1–5 in book 1, or what? If this book is regulated in terms of 'balance', is that anything to do with the pattern of 'Horse and Cart' Chapter headings, 'Copula + Copula' as we might dub it, twinned Ways of Being? Do 'Women and Sex' fit like 'Greek and the Greeks' or is there some other form of 'balance' here? Is 'balance' one of those self-justifying operators? Can it work when you are dealing with *Satire*? Is the violation of the principle which makes the former member of the other five pairs one syllable *shorter* than the latter ('Aims and Motives' to 'Greek and the-Greeks': contrast 'Women and Sex') an accident, a rhetorically-determined or substantive decision? It makes a difference to *me*. I'm afraid I shall have to have returned to this whole problematic in my text above. Meantime, does R call what he has 'learned . . . from critical writing over the last thirty-odd years' *'opinions'*—just five quickfire opinions across a half page—because he's being charmingly self-deprecating, in a traditional human-ist kind of way, or is it that he despairs of persuading anyone that there's any more to all this *critical writing* than 'opinions'? Realise that R is here binding all the years he has devoted to Roman Satire and to reading criticism into his reading of Roman Satire—, 'Above all else, Roman Satire is about Roman life' is 'opinion' no. 1—but when R says he 'has learned something, he hopes, from various kinds of critical writing over the last thirty-odd years', you must wonder whether he's being roguishly 'literary'— satirical, indeed—when you realise that he *just* hasn't told you that he's read any criticism written in those 'odd' years and he may have told you, *if* he has told you this, that what he has learned from that criticism is *just* that the 'truisms within the humanist tradition' are 'widely contested' outside it. In other words, 'behind' his book in this preface *could* be a claim to have learned nothing from the critical writings produced in the best years of his life. I would like to know whether R learned to include a chapter on 'Women and Sex' from recent critical writings: or was there a 'traditional humanist' 'opinion' behind *that*? If so, was it the traditional or was it the humanist bit of the opinion that made him put sex down as six, put women down as l(e)ast, couple 'Women' with 'Sex' and suppose it didn't need even an 'opinion' to go with, or 'behind', it? (The missing sixth column.) This is all ironically rich. Indeed, if R's traditional opinions *are* the same *even* thirty years on, they're ironically rich.

Both their contestation 'outside' humanism and the living of a life must have *somewhat* altered their meanings, however successfully their wordings may have defied change. Anyhow, isn't it *worth* producing the justification for these traditional 'opinions' *in* the book, where it belongs, up front, not 'behind' it, where you might risk learning nothing from them and where, as things stand, you cannot learn what it is that R *has* learned, that 'something' he mentions, from recent critical writings? Of course this is a 'Themes' book, indeed it's a 'horizontal' Student Textbook: too practical for Theory, no doubt. 'Opinions' *is* another self-justifying operator. Isn't it? It goes together with 'Themes', so: 'Themes and Opinions', the chapter 'behind' the book that ought to just-if-y the opinion *'Women and Sex'* . . .

8. Weedon 1987, 102.
9. See Kappeler 1986, 108.
10. McConnell & McConnell in Armstrong & Tennenhouse 1987, 208.
11. Greene & Kahn 1985b, 22.
12. Greene & Kahn 1985a, 6, Weedon 1987, 167.
13. For this distinction between a 'given', bodily, physical, physiological, natural (socially-produced) 'sexuality' and an elaborated, displaced, constructed, cultural 'gender' see Caplan 1987, Introd. 1f., Connell 1987 *passim*.
14. References are to the fragments and translations as in the Loeb of Warmington 1979.
15. Rudd 1986, 10.
16. Anderson 1982, 21.
17. Williams 1968, 452.
18. Coffey 1976, 45.
19. Weedon 1987, 78ff. esp. 88, 173.
20. Ramage, Sigsbee & Fredericks 1974, 2.
21. Pollock 1988, 67.
22. Cf. Anderson 1982, 34, Coffey 1976, 51.
23. Ramage & co 1974, 40.
24. Coffey 1976, 52.
25. Pollock 1988, 67.
26. Moi 1985, 8.
27. Henderson 1989.
28. Richlin 1981, 42. Cf. Veyne 1987, 204, etc.
29. Anderson 1982, 3.
30. See esp. Kenney 1962. Cf. Harrison 1987, etc.
31. Anderson 1982, Introd. viii.
32. See Hor. *Sat.* 1.4.105ff., 1.6 and Armstrong 1986. My account is greatly influenced by Zetzel 1980, esp. 68f. At 1.6.55ff., Virgil plays midwife-cum-elder sibling (not 'Big Brother'!): Virgil's *Bucolica* present a 'Treaty of Brundisium' in ten hexameter pieces for Pollio; Horace's first book treads in his marks to produce his 'Treaty of Tarentum' for Maecenas, cf. Van Rooy 1973. All the difference in the world, the two worlds they create . . . I shall be

using for H the exemplary translation by Rudd, along with some of his annotations (1973). I advise you to do so, too.

33. This term is now in common use: e.g. Weedon 1987, 66, Jones in Greene & Kahn 1985a, 81; see esp. Gallop 1982, 15f.

34. On this poem I follow Curran 1970.

35. Anderson 1982, 38.

36. Vessey 1976.

37. Bushala 1971.

38. Williams 1972, 17, 18.

39. I am quoting from the Oxford Latin Dictionary here.

40. I cite this from Lewis & Short.

41. See McConnell & McConnell in Armstrong & Tennenhouse 1987 on this.

42. On this poem see Anderson 1982, 74f. For Priapus see Richlin 1983, just about the only work on Roman Satire to work with feminist knowledge. Ideally you need to read Richlin 1984.

43. Rudd 1982, 72.

44. On 'Canidia' you could read my essay on Horace, *Epode* 8, Henderson 1987 esp. 112f. But it's *very* rude, I suppose . . .

45. McConnell & McConnell in Armstrong & Tennenhouse 1987, 212. Cf. *ib.* 234 'Women must *pretend* to be women so that men can be thought of as *real*'. Do you recognise this?

46. Cf. Armstrong 1986, 279f. Read Satires 2.3.247f., 2.5.74f., 2.7.46f. with the questions you 'learned' from 1.2 in mind.

47. E.g. Kilpatrick 1986, Introd. xxi ff.

48. Bramble 1974 is the best book on gender in Latin Literature. I shall use Guy Lee's brilliant translations of P in Lee & Barr 1987.

49. See Foucault 1988, 64f.

50. I really must warn you of a sexual/textual crotch/crux here: the MSS give, in the translation of Rudd 1973, 'What a way to behave, weeding your privates and the recesses of your rump, displaying your shrivelled *vulva* to the public!' Which of us has got the biggest buzz from this? P writing it? Roman students reading it? Roman teachers teaching it? Modern editors collating, justifying or emending it? Housman conj(ect)uring *ualuas*, 'doors' or Richter *bulbos*, 'onions'? Translators re-writing it? You and I poring over it? Or should we (all) get the *least* buzz we *can* from our *vulvas*, *valvas* or *bulbos*?

51. A phrase from Strenski 1987, 143.

52. In default of a really good translation, I use Robinson 1983 here. Ferguson 1979 is a really *useful* text-plus-commentary.

53. Anderson 1982, 296.

54. On J 2 see Braund & Cloud 1981, 203f.

55. See Smith 1980 for a way to read J 6. You should read Loraux 1987 1.2 where she brilliantly deconstructs the logic of the infamous vituperation of women as a 'race' in Semonides frag. 7. (Cf. Lefkowitz & Fant (1982) no. 30.)

56. Foucault 1988, 185f. Cf. Veyne 1987, 36f.

57. Zeitlin in Burian 1985, 56: a brilliant essay about the Self.
58. On this poem see Braund 1988, ch. 4.
59. Ferguson 1979, 248. Compare his introduction to J 6 (185): 'J's misogyny does not allow any but bad women . . . In his first book J showed little interest in women . . . He now makes up for lost time'. A different tone altogether? Anything to do with *gender*, do you think?
60. Ferguson 1979, 248.
61. Thanks to Dr E.L.Morris in the School of Engineering of Exeter University for his help in making compatible two incompatible floppy disks. (*Ed.*)

Bibliography

Thanks to Professor Niall Rudd of Bristol University for permission to use his excellent Penguin translation of Horace and Persius, (1979, reprinted with revisions 1987) *Horace: Satires and Epistles and Persius: Satires*

Anderson L. 1982, *Big science* (Warner Bros. Records)
Anderson W.S. 1982, *Essays on Roman Satire*
André J. 1981 (2nd ed.), *L'Alimentation et la Cuisine à Rome*
Armstrong D. 1986, 'Horatius *eques et scriba*: Satires 1.6 and 2.7' *TAPhA* 116 255–88
Armstrong N. & Tennenhouse, L. 1987 (edd.) *The ideology of conduct. Essays in literature and the history of sexuality*

Balsdon J.P.V.D. 1969, *Life and Leisure in Ancient Rome*
Becker W.A. 1868 (8th English ed.), *Gallus*
Borges J.L. 1970, *Labyrinths*
Bramble J.C. 1974, *Persius and the programmatic satire. A study in form and imagery*
Braund S.H. 1988, *Beyond Anger: A Study of Juvenal's third Book of Satires*
Braund S.H. & Cloud J.D. 1981, 'Juvenal: a diptych' *LCM* 6 195–208
Brink C. 1982, *Horace on Poetry: Epistles Book II*
Bruns K.G. & Gradenwitz O. 1909, *Fontes Iuris Romani Antiqui* (7th ed.)
Buckland W.W. & Stein P. 1963, *A Text-book of Roman Law from Augustus to Justinian* (3rd ed.)
Burian P. 1985 (ed.), *Directions in Euripidean criticism*
Bushala E.W. 1971, 'The motif of sexual choice in Horace, Satire 1,2' *CJ* 66 312–5
Butler H.E. 1909, *Post-Augustan Poetry*

Caplan P. 1987 (ed.,) *The cultural construction of sexuality*
Carcopino J. 1962 (tr.), *Daily Life in Ancient Rome*
Cavenaile P. 1958, *Corpus Papyrorum Latinorum I–IV*

Classen C.J. 1978, 'Horace—a cook?' *CQ* 28 333–48
Cloud J.D. 1989, 'The client-patron relationship: emblem and reality in Juvenal's First Book', in Wallace-Hadrill A. (ed.) *Patronage in Ancient Society*, 205–18
Coffey M. 1976, *Roman Satire*
Colton R.C. 1964, 'Dinner invitation: Juvenal 11.56–208' *CB* 16 39–45
Connell R.W. 1987, *Gender and power. Societies, the person and sexual politics*

Courtney E. 1980, *A commentary on the satires of Juvenal*
Crook J.A. 1967, *Law and Life of Rome*
Crook J.A. 1973, 'Intestacy in Roman Society' *PCPhS* 199 38–44
Curran L.C. 1970, 'Nature, convention, and obscenity in Horace, Satires 1.2' *Arion*
    9 220–45

Daube D. 1965, 'Intestacy at Rome', *Tulane Law Review* 39 253–62
Dessen C.S. 1968, *Iunctura Callidus Acri*
Dixon S. 1985, 'Breaking the law to do the right thing', *Adelaide Law Review* 9
    519–34
Dixon S. 1988, *The Roman Mother*
Durry M. 1935, 'Juvénal et les prétoriens' *REL* 13 95–106

Ehrenberg V. & Jones A.H.M. 1976 (2nd ed.), *Documents illustrating the reigns of*
    Augustus and Tiberius

Felton K. & Lee K.H. 1972, 'The theme of Juvenal's eleventh satire' *Latomus*
    1041–6
Ferguson J. 1979, *Juvenal. The Satires*
Flower B. & Rosenbaum E. 1958, *Apicius: The Roman cookery book*
Foucault M. 1984 (repr. 1988), *The care of the self. The history of sexuality. Volume*
    3
Fraenkel E. 1957, *Horace*
Frayn J. 1979, *Subsistence farming in Roman Italy*
Fruelund Jensen B. 1986, 'Martyred and beleaguered virtue: Juvenal's portrait of
    Umbricius' *C & M* 37 185–97

Gallop J. 1982, *Feminism and Psychoanalysis. The daughter's seduction*
Gardner J.F. 1986, *Women in Roman Law and Society*
Garnsey P. & Saller R. 1987, *The Roman empire: economy, society and culture*
Gérard J. 1976, *Juvénal et la réalité contemporaine*
Girard P.F. & Senn F. 1977, *Textes de droit romain II* (7th ed.)
Gratwick A.S. 1982, 'The satires of Ennius and Lucilius' in Kenney E.J. & Clausen
    W.V. (edd.) *The Cambridge History of Classical Literature II: Latin Literature*,
    156–71
Green P. 1960, *Essays in Antiquity*
Greene, G. & Kahn, C. 1985a (edd.), *Making a difference. Feminist literary criticism*
Greene G. & Kahn C. 1985b, 'Feminist scholarship and the social construction of
    woman', in Greene & Kahn 1985a, 1–36
Grellet-Dumazeau M. 1858 (repr. 1972), *Le Barreau Romain*

Harrison G. 1987, 'The confessions of Lucilius (Horace Sat.2.1.30–34): a defense
    of autobiographical satire?' *CA* 6 38–52

Henderson J. 1987, 'Suck it and see (Horace, *Epode* 8)', in Whitby M., Hardie P. & Whitby M. 1987 (edd.), *Homo Viator. Classical Essays for John Bramble*, 105–18

Henderson J. 1989, 'Satire writes 'Woman': Gendersong' *PCPhS* 215 (forthcoming)

Highet G. 1954, *Juvenal the Satirist*

Highet G. 1962, *The Anatomy of Satire*

Hodgart M. 1969, *Satire*

Jenkinson J.R. 1980, *Persius, The Satires*

Jones A.R. 1985, 'Inscribing femininity: French theories of the feminine', in Greene & Kahn 1985a, 80–112

Johnston D. 1988, *The Roman Law of Trusts*

Johnston D. 1989, 'Justinian's Digest: the interpretation of interpolation', *Oxford Journal of Legal Studies* (forthcoming)

Kappeler S. 1986, *The pornography of representation*

Kelly J.M. 1966, *Roman Litigation*

Kennedy D.F. 1984, Review of Woodman T. & West D. *Poetry and politics in the age of Augustus* (1984), *LCM* 9 157–60

Kenney E.J. 1962, 'The First Satire of Juvenal' *PCPhS* 8 29–40

Kenney E.J. 1971, *Lucretius De Rerum Natura Book III*

Kernan A. 1959, *The Cankered Muse: Satire of the English Renaissance*

Kilpatrick R.S. 1986, *The poetry of friendship. Horace, Epistles 1*

LaFleur R.A. 1979, '*Amicitia* and the unity of Juvenal's first book' *ICS* 4 158–77

Leach E.W. 1974, *Vergil's Eclogues. Landscapes of Experience*

Lee G. & Barr W. 1987, *The Satires of Persius*

Leeman A.D. 1982, 'Rhetorical Status in Horace Serm. 2.1', in Vickers B. (ed.) *Rhetoric Revalued*, 159–63

Leeman A.D. 1983, 'Die Konsultierung des Trebatius: Statuslehre in Horaz, Serm. 2,1', in Händel P. & Meid W. (edd.) *Festschrift R. Muth*, 209–15

Lefkowitz M.R. & Fant M.B. 1982, *Women's life in Greece & Rome. A source book in translation*

Loraux, N. 1981 (repr. 1987), *The children of Athena*

McConnell D. & McConnell J.F. 1987, 'The beauty system', in Armstrong & Tennenhouse 1987, 206–38

Maguinness W.S. 1938, 'Friends and philosophy of friendship in Horace' *Hermathena* 51 29–48

Marongiu A. 1977, 'Giovenale e il diritto', *SDHI* 43 167–87

Mennell, S. 1985, *All manners of food*

Moi, T. 1985, *Sexual/textual politics*

Morford, M. 1977, 'Juvenal's fifth satire' *AJPh* 98 219–45

Van Morrison 1984, *A sense of wonder* (Mercury Records)
Motto A.L. & Clark J.R. 1965, '*Per iter tenebricosum*: The Mythos of Juvenal 3'
    TAPhA 96 267–76
Murray O. 1983, 'The Greek Symposium in History', in Gabba, E. (ed.) *Tria
    Corda: Scritta in Onore di Arnaldo Momigliano*, 257-72

Nettleship H. 1895, *Lectures and essays*
Nisbet R.G.M. 1963, 'Persius', in Sullivan J.P. (ed.) *Critical essays on Roman
    literature: satire*, 39–71

Paoli U.E. 1963 (tr.), *Rome: its people, life and customs*
Paratore E. 1964, 'Ad Hor. Serm. 1.9.35–42 e 74–78', in Guarino A. & Labruna
    L. (edd.) *Synteleia (Studi Arangio-Ruiz)* 2, 828–48
Pollock G. 1988, *Vision & difference. Femininity, feminism and the histories of art*

Ramage E.S., Sigsbee D.L. & Fredericks S.C. 1974, *Roman Satirists and their satire.
    The fine art of criticism in ancient Rome*
Richlin A. 1981, 'The meaning of *irrumare* in Catullus and Martial' *CPh* 76 40–6
Richlin A. 1983, *The garden of Priapus. Sexuality and aggression in Roman humor*
Richlin A. 1984, 'Invective against women in Roman satire' *Arethusa* 17 67–80
Robinson S. 1983, *Juvenal. Sixteen Satires upon the ancient harlot*
Rudd, N. 1966, *The Satires of Horace*
Rudd, N. 1986, *Themes in Roman satire*

Sherwin-White A.N. 1966, *The Letters of Pliny: a historical and social commentary*
Smith R.E. 1951, 'The Law of Libel at Rome', *CQ* 1 169–79
Smith W.S. Jr. 1980, 'Husband vs. wife in Juvenal's sixth satire' *CW* 73 323–32
Steiner W. 1982, *The Colors of rhetoric. Problems in the relation between modern
    literature and painting*
Strenski I. 1987, *Four theories of myth in twentieth-century history. Cassirer, Eliade,
    Lévi-Strauss and Malinowski*
Syme R. 1958, *Tacitus*
Syme R. 1986, *The Augustan Aristocracy*

Townend G.B. 1973, 'The literary substrata to Juvenal's Satires', *JRS* 63 148–60

Van Rooy C.A. 1973, '*Imitatio* of Vergil, *Eclogues* in Horace, *Satires* book 1' *AClass*
    16 69–88
Vessey D.W.T. 1976, 'A note on *latus*' *LCM* 1 39–40
Veyne P. 1987 (ed.), *A history of private life, volume 1*

Walford E. 1875, *Juvenal*
Walsh P.G. 1970, *The Roman Novel*

Warde Fowler W. 1908, *Social life at Rome in the age of Cicero*

Warmington E.H. 1938, *Remains of Old Latin, volume 3: Lucilius; the Twelve Tables*

Watson A. 1971, *The Law of Succession in the Later Roman Republic*

Weedon, C. 1987, *Feminist practice & poststructuralist theory*

Weisinger K. 1972, 'Irony and moderation in Juvenal XI' *CSCA* 5 227–40

West D. 1974, 'Of Mice and Men: Horace, *Satires* 2.6.77–117' in Woodman T. & West D. (edd.) *Quality and Pleasure in Latin Poetry*, 67–80

White P. 1978, '*Amicitia* and the profession of poetry' *JRS* 68 74–92

Williams G. 1968, *Tradition and originality in Roman poetry*

Williams G. 1972, *Horace (Greece & Rome New Surveys in the Classics* No. 6)

Williams F. 1984, '*Vox clamantis in theatro* (Juvenal 3, 153)', in Cairns F. (ed.) *Liverpool Latin Seminar Vol. 4*, 121–7

Wolf J.G. 1985, 'Das sogenannte Ladungsvadimonium', in Ankum J.A., Spruit J.E. & Wubbe F.B.J. (edd.) *Satura R. Feenstra*, 59–69

Zeitlin F.I. 1985, 'The power of Aphrodite: Eros and the boundaries of the self in the *Hippolytus*', in Burian 1985, 52–110

Zetzel J.E.G. 1980, 'Horace's *Liber sermonum*: the structure of ambiguity' *Arethusa* 13 59–77

Notes on Contributors

Dr Susan Braund teaches in the Department of Classics at the University of Exeter. Her research interests are particularly in the field of Roman Satire. She has recently published a monograph entitled *Beyond Anger: A Study of Juvenal's third Book of Satires* (1988) and is preparing a commentary on Juvenal Book I (Satires 1-5) for C.U.P.

Dr Roland Mayer teaches in the Department of Classics at King's College, London University. He specialises in Roman literature and thought and is currently preparing a commentary on Horace *Epistles* I for C.U.P. His publications include commentaries on Lucan Civil War Book 8 (1981) and on Seneca *Phaedra* (1990).

Duncan Cloud teaches in the Department of Classics at Leicester University. His research interests embrace Roman Law (on which he has published numerous articles), Roman history and Roman Satire. He is a contributor to the revised *Cambridge Ancient History*.

Nicola Hudson is a graduate of Exeter University and is completing her Ph.D. in the Department of Classics at Leicester University. Her thesis has as its title 'Food: a suitable subject for satire'.

Dr John Henderson teaches Classics at King's College, Cambridge University. He has published a number of challenging articles which employ contemporary critiques to explore Latin Literature within the frame of Roman culture.